People of the Ancient World

THE ANCIENT EGYPTIANS

WRITTEN BY
LILA PERL

Franklin Watts
A Division of Scholastic Inc.
New York Toronto London Auckland Sydney
Mexico City New Delhi Hong Kong
Danbury, Connecticut

Note to readers: Definitions for words in **bold** can be found in the Glossary at the back of this book.

Photographs © 2004: Art Resource, NY: 22 (Giraudon), 26 (Erich Lessing), 41, 97 bottom (Scala), 73 (Werner Forman); Bridgeman Art Library International Ltd., London/New York: 47 (Ancient Art and Architecture Collection Ltd.), 60 (Bonhams, London, UK), 64 (British Museum, London UK), 13, 17 (Deir el-Medina, Thebes, Egypt), 91, 97 top (Egyptian National Museum, Cairo, Egypt), 15, 59 (Giraudon), 35 (Saqqara, Egypt), 65 (Werner Forman); Corbis Images: 32 bottom (Archivo Iconografico, S.A.), 92 left, 94 top, 99 top (Gianni Dagli Orti), 7, 8 (Reuters New-Media Inc.), 51 (Lee Snider), 75 (Sandro Vannini), 70, 90 top right, 96 (Roger Wood); Digital Stock via SODA: 54, 98; National Geographic Image Collection: 95 (Kenneth Garrett), 57 (Christopher A. Klein); Nik Wheeler: 6, 11, 87; North Wind Picture Archives: 50; Peter Arnold Inc./Malcolm S. Kirk: 37, 44; Stone/Getty Images/Stephen Studd: 4; Superstock, Inc./Silvio Fiori: 90 top left, 100; The Art Archive/Picture Desk: 33, 84, 85 (Dagli Orti), 32 top, 39, 62, 67, 72, 90 bottom, 94 bottom, 99 bottom (Dagli Orti/Egyptian Museum Cairo), 23 (Dagli Orti/Egyptian Museum Turin), 19, 38, 92 right, 94 top (Dagli Orti/Musee du Louvre, Paris), 81, 82 (Dagli Orti/Ragab Papyrus Institute Cairo); The British Museum: 77; The Image Works: 14, 27, 28, 76, 79, 86 (The British Museum/Topham-HIP), 43, 49 (Topham).

Cover art by Richard Deurer
Map by XNR Productions Inc.
Pyramid diagrams by Robert Cronan

Library of Congress Cataloging-in-Publication Data

Perl, Lila
  The ancient Egyptians / by Lila Perl.
    p. cm. — (People of the ancient world)
Includes bibliographical references and index.
ISBN 0-531-12345-6 (lib. bdg.)   0-531-16738-0 (pbk.)
1. Egypt—Civilization—to 332 B.C.—Juvenile literature. I. Title. II. Series.
DT61.P45 2004
932—dc22

                                                            2004001940

Contents

HOW WE KNOW ABOUT ANCIENT EGYPT

All too often,
the peoples of
the past have left
us scanty and mysti-
fying clues as to how
they lived, worked, and
died. The cave paintings,
tools, and pottery of prehistoric
humans, for example, do not tell
us a connected story. A great deal of
information about their daily lives is left
to our imagination.

By stark contrast, the people of ancient
Egypt have given us a vivid picture of their lives
over the course of their three-thousand-year history. Principal among their offerings are their massive
stone monuments—pyramids, temples, statuary, and
tombs—ordered to be built by generations of rulers who
sought to be remembered through eternity.

We can learn about the ancient Egyptians by studying what their civilization left behind. These sculptures were found in Luxor, Egypt.

We learn, too, from these memorials—which are remarkably well preserved due to Egypt's consistently warm, dry climate—that the everyday people of Egypt were master builders. They labored in an age when only stone, copper, or bronze hand tools were available. As a result, the making of immense structures had to be accomplished through careful planning and human physical power.

The culture and creativity of the ancient Egyptians have been preserved in even greater detail due to their custom of placing everyday objects, ornaments, jewelry, musical instruments, games, and similar items in the tombs of their rulers and other high-ranking members of society. Here, too, credit must be given to the artisans, craftspeople, and sculptors who fashioned these treasured articles.

The burial places of the mighty—and, as time passed, the lesser members of society—were designed to provide the deceased with all the necessities and pleasures they had known in life. The purpose of this custom was to enable the dead to live eternally in what the Egyptians envisioned as the afterlife. The tomb contents of ancient Egypt, like the structures in which they were found, have proven to be gifts to posterity of beauty and knowledge.

The same is true for the walls of the tombs themselves, many of which are painted and sculpted with vividly colored scenes from numerous aspects of Egyptian life. Again, because of the dry climate of Egypt, the decorated walls are well preserved and fresh-looking. They tell us about such daily pursuits as fishing, farming, and hunting. They portray banquets and entertainments, religious rituals, warriors and their captives, and finally death itself, with depictions of the process of mummification and of tearful funeral processions.

Additional testimony to the lives of the ancient Egyptians is derived from their written language, a system of **hieroglyphics** that, once it was deciphered by scholars, has revealed a great amount of information. Translations of the ancient Egyptian language include, among many other things, royal decrees, the workings of government, victories in battle, poems, songs, stories, and prayers for the dead.

Finally, enormous evidence of the past has been collected through the painstaking work of explorers, archaeologists, scholars, and scientists, who have made ancient Egypt their special area of investigation. Among their discoveries, for example, have

Archaeologists examine the walls of a tomb near the pyramid of Sakkara. Much of what we know of ancient Egypt comes from wall carvings and paintings.

been human mummies, thousands of years old, the ages and medical histories of which have been scientifically determined. Modern science has even been able to provide chemical analyses of many of the foods, plants, ointments, and other substances found in the tombs.

The work of the Egyptologists has not reached its end. On the contrary, excavations and examinations of the ancient past continue, revealing both newly discovered tomb sites and yet more settlement sites.

These findings offer us ongoing information about a people who lived lives that were, for the most part, both orderly and creative. Egyptian civilization, with its stability, productivity, and prolonged periods of peace with its neighbors, can teach us lessons and impart values to which all modern nations might aspire.

On a more personal level, the people of ancient Egypt communicate to us the virtues of work, family, love of learning, respect for knowledge, and such a tenacious regard for life that they sought to prolong it after death.

An expert in ancient artifacts inspects a sarcophagus in a newly discovered tomb in Egypt.

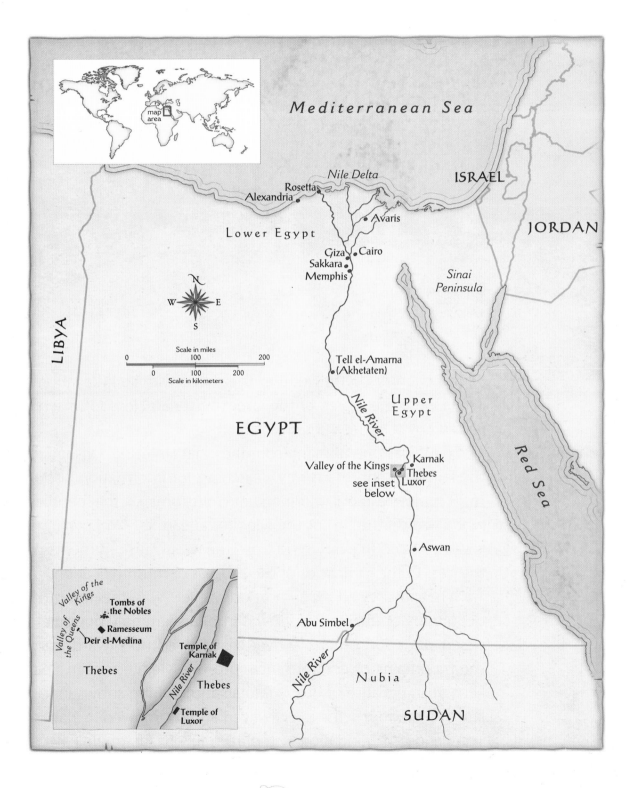

Mediterranean Sea

map area

ISRAEL

JORDAN

Nile Delta

Rosetta
Alexandria

Avaris

Lower Egypt

Giza
Sakkara
Memphis

Cairo

Sinai
Peninsula

N
W   E
S

Scale in miles
0   100   200

0   100   200
Scale in kilometers

LIBYA

Tell el-Amarna
(Akhetaten)

Upper
Egypt

EGYPT

Nile River

Red Sea

Valley of the Kings
see inset
below

Karnak
Thebes
Luxor

Aswan

Abu Simbel

Nile River

Nubia

SUDAN

Valley of the
Kings

Tombs of
the Nobles

Valley of
the Queens

Ramesseum

Deir el-Medina

Temple of
Karnak

Thebes

Thebes

Nile River

Temple of
Luxor

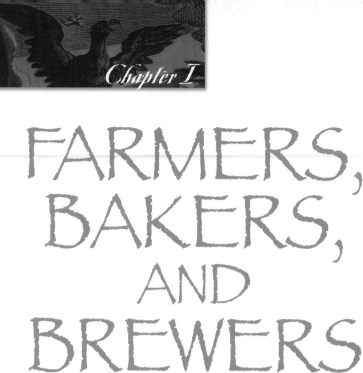

Chapter I

FARMERS, BAKERS, AND BREWERS

The Nile River provided the much-needed water to make farming possible in an otherwise arid land.

"In no country do they gather their seed with so little labor." These were the words of the Greek historian Herodotus who visited Egypt in the 400s B.C.

Egypt was one of many countries that Herodotus visited in the known world of his day, searching for information about the history, religion, manners, and customs of the peoples who lived on the rim of the Mediterranean Sea. In Egypt, he was interested in everything from the massive monuments of the past to the intricacies of the process of mummification.

What impressed him most, however, was the amazing geography of the land. In the heart of a seemingly boundless desert ran a long, narrow river that flowed northward from the mountains of central Africa into the Mediterranean Sea. Each year, because of heavy rainfall and melting snows in the lands to the south, the river swelled and overflowed its banks. The period of inundation lasted from July to October, leaving a deposit of fresh silt that eventually transformed the dry

sands into fertile land on which grains, vegetables, flax, and other basic necessities of a settled farming life could be grown. The great river, the Nile, more than 4,000 miles (6,400 kilometers) in length, made it possible for human beings to thrive in the very midst of a lifeless desert. For this reason, Herodotus called the Egypt that he visited, "A gift of the Nile."

Farming Along the Nile

The recorded history of ancient Egypt goes all the way back to 3100 B.C. But it was well before that date—probably as long ago as 5000 B.C. or earlier —that the first farmers of the Neolithic, or New Stone Age, began to settle on the banks of the Nile. The Nile valley, in that era, is believed to have been wetter than it was at the time of Herodotus. Huge marshes on either side of the river supported such large animals as hippopotamuses and antelopes as well as cranes and a variety of other wading birds. Gradually, however, the hunters and food gatherers of the marshes turned to farming the rich black land of the riverbanks. The desert beyond the riverbanks became known as the red land.

The beginning of a settled farming life along the Nile signaled the development of the great civilization that was to come. For without a reliable agricultural base, no society in the ancient world could have flourished. In Egypt, there would have been no priests and no pantheon of the gods to bestow, among other benefits, good harvests. There would have been no great rulers and no lasting monuments of the kind that mark the long-lived civilization that arose.

The food crops that grew best in the black land were wheat and barley. The wheat was of a variety known as emmer, a hard red grain that was difficult to refine. These two grains, made into bread and beer, formed the staples of the ordinary Egyptian's

A wall painting shows ancient Egyptians harvesting their crops.

diet. The vegetables grown in ancient Egypt included beans, peas, lentils, onions, garlic, radishes, cucumbers, and lettuce.

For the wealthier classes, grapes were grown and pressed into wine. Fruits, such as dates, figs, and pomegranates, were eaten at festival times and at funerals. Honey, from wild or domesticated bees, was used to sweeten cakes and, along with dates, the thick beer the Egyptians drank.

Cattle were raised to provide meat and milk, and also to carry heavy loads or perform other difficult work. Goats, sheep, wild game, ducks, geese, and other waterfowl were also sources of meat. But except for festival days or funeral feasts, only upper-class

The ancient Egyptians raised cattle to use as food as well as to help them with their work.

Egyptians are believed to have had meat in their diets. There is, however, recent evidence that meat was provided in relatively large quantities to the workers who built the pyramids at Giza.

Fish, on the other hand, was a food of the poor, although certain varieties were considered taboo for religious reasons. Such fish were believed to have devoured parts of the body of the god Osiris when, according to legend, his body was cut into pieces and thrown into the Nile. Because of the hot Egyptian climate, much of the fish caught in the Nile was salted in order to preserve it.

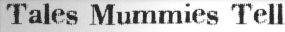

Tales Mummies Tell

We know a great deal about the diet of the ancient Egyptians from the paintings on the walls of their tombs and from funerary models. The latter were miniature three-dimensional scenes carved from stone or wood, which show men and women producing food and drink, butchering cattle, hunting ducks, and harpooning fish. These funerary models were placed inside the tombs. The wall paintings and replicas also show us wheat being threshed, beer being brewed, cattle and other animals for the tables of the wealthy being force-fed, and grapes being picked for wine.

However, modern-day examinations of the teeth of **mummies** found in the tombs tell us something more. All Egyptians, including those of the upper classes, were found to have teeth that were ground down, in some cases almost to the gums, causing painful infections. Why was this so?

Bread was the staple food of Egypt. But the grain from which it was made was coarse and difficult to refine. Also, it was milled into flour between stones that shed fine particles, as well as sand and other grit. As even the greatest Egyptian ruler chewed on the baked loaf set before him, he gradually ground his teeth to stumps, a secret he would take to his tomb and that only his mummy would disclose.

Lives of Egyptian Farmers

The homes of the simplest Nile farmers were made of reeds or, more often, of mud bricks, a mixture of mud and straw shaped in molds and baked in the sun. Houses were usually one story high with stairs leading to a flat roof, which could be used for storage and as a place to rest after the heat of the day. Pens for animals were attached to the dwellings. Although Herodotus wrote of Egyptian farming as requiring "little labor," the rituals and rigors of the farming year were highly demanding.

After the four-month period of inundation known as Akhet, during which the Nile overflowed its banks, came the four-month planting and growing season of Peret. Cattle were used to pull the shallow wooden plows and to trample the seed into the ground. Once the seeds of barley and emmer wheat sprouted, the crops had to be watered, for there would be no rainfall in the desert climate of the Nile valley during the four-month drought of Shemu, which followed Peret. Thus a network of canals and irrigation ditches had to be maintained by the farmers through-out the cultivated land. The Nile farmers kept busy, too, weeding the fields and keeping them free of birds and insects attracted by the growing crops. At the end of Shemu, the crops were harvested.

When the grain was ready to be harvested, it was cut with wooden sickles that had flint teeth embedded in them. The Egyptians had no iron for field tools. Threshing, or separating the seed of the grain from the straw, was accomplished by having the farmer's oxen trample the harvested grain. Winnowing was the next step. Men, women, and children came out to the fields to toss the grain in the air to separate the seed coverings and other debris, known as the chaff, from the seed itself.

The Egyptian farming year had now come full cycle. It consisted of twelve thirty-day months, with an additional five days at the end of the year to make 365. The Egyptian priests soon added an extra quarter day every year, matching the present-day calendar (to which we add an extra day every fourth year). Historians believe that this lunar calendar was adopted as early as 2800 B.C.

There was also an Egyptian solar calendar, which was keyed to the rising of the star Sirius, the brightest star in the heavens, known as the Dog Star. Both calendars were in use at the same time.

Although the new year, which began with the Nile flood—and corresponded to our July—was considered to be a time of rest, it was actually one of preparation during which tools were mended, boundaries were marked, and irrigation channels had to be repaired. It was also a time for tallying up the returns of the harvest and for paying taxes.

As the basis of the Egyptian economy, agriculture came to be practiced on a more elaborate scale with the passage of time. People who acquired wealth, such as government officials, established their own farming estates on which tenant farmers lived and worked, as did other specialized laborers, artisans, scribes, and house servants.

Each estate functioned like a small town. Although built of mud brick like the houses of the poorer farmers, the estate buildings were usually coated with plaster and their inner walls were colorfully decorated. The estates also had their own bakeries and breweries.

Bread was made with flour, yeast, salt, and water. The dough was kneaded by hand, shaped into loaves, left to rise, and then baked in small clay ovens. Sometimes Egyptian bread was baked in pottery molds of which examples have been found at various sites. Fermented barley was the basis of Egyptian beer, which was not high in alcoholic content and, with the addition of honey and dates, was sweet and fairly nutritious. It tended, however, to be lumpy in consistency. It was usually drunk through a straw, fashioned from a plant fiber that had a hollow tubelike center.

A sculpture depicts workers grinding grain to make bread and beer. Bread and beer were important parts of the Egyptian diet.

Farming estates might also cultivate their own flax, the hardy plant that grew along the Nile and from which linen was spun and woven. Cotton was unknown during much of ancient Egyptian history, and garments of wool, from animal fleece, were coarse and itchy in the heat. Many Egyptians considered wool unclean.

Flax fiber could be spun and woven into materials ranging from strong rope to a fine, transparent fabric that could be draped and fashionably pleated by the ladies of the royal court. The Nile farmers, as well as other members of the laboring classes, wore kilts of medium-weight linen, while women who worked in the fields and as household servants wore straight, sheathlike garments of the same material.

Wives on the Farms and Estates

Marriage appears to have been a revered institution in ancient Egypt. The romantic poetry of the Egyptians and the many statues of loyal and contented married couples seem to attest to this. "Start your household and love your wife," young men were advised. "Fill her stomach with food and provide clothes for her back. Make her heart glad as long as you live." Even though most marriages were probably arranged, there may also have been a fairly high degree of choice in selecting a mate.

Women of all classes married young, probably around the age of fourteen. Men tended to be five or six years older. Most importantly, even the poorest farmers' wives had a remarkable amount of independence. The were allowed to maintain control of any assets they brought to the marriage. They could inherit property, and they could buy and sell it as they pleased.

Almost throughout Egyptian history, especially during the period known as the New Kingdom, women were reported to have borne witness in court cases and to have taken their own grievances before a judge. There is even one record of women having served as judges. On the farming estates, it was not unusual for a woman to manage the affairs of the household and farm. Women also worked outside the home, as servants, musicians, priestesses, and as hired mourners at funerals. While the spinning and weaving of linen were mainly household occupations, there were also instances of women being employed outside the home as weavers of cloth.

The strong position of women in Egyptian society undoubtedly reinforced its stability, its success, and its thousands of years of endurance.

Chapter II

PRIESTS
AND
SCRIBES

Natural phenomena were mysteries to the ancient Egyptians. They marveled at the daily cycle of the rising of the sun, they watched the night skies for the phases of the moon and the movement of the stars, and most intently they waited each year for the flooding of the Nile. How were they to explain these events? They believed that they resulted from the actions of kindly, beneficent gods.

The growers of crops gave names and distinct images to the gods of nature. The god of the sun was called Ra (or Re) and was represented as having a human body with the head of a falcon. Atop the falcon's head was a disk that symbolized the sun. Equally important to the farmers was the Nile god, Hapi (sometimes seen on carvings as a pair of gods of similar appearance). Hapi had a human head and a thickset body, representing the abundance that the Nile brought forth when it overflowed its banks. Water lily and papyrus plants, which grew in the shallows of the river, were sometimes portrayed as sprouting from the river god's head.

A stele (carved stone) shows a woman appearing before Ra, the god of the sun.

Priests, Servants of the Gods

Numerous other gods were worshipped by the Egyptians, all of them through the intermediary offices of the priests, who were known as "the servants of the gods" and who had immense power and influence throughout Egyptian history. Priests could marry and have children but were sworn to lives of cleanliness and honesty. They shaved their heads and bodies and dressed in fine white linen, presided in the great stone temples dedicated to the gods, officiated at religious ceremonies and festivals, and played an all-important role at funerals, especially those of Egypt's great rulers.

The appointment of a high priest by the royal house was an event of great importance. "Nebunef has been named high priest of Amun [also Amen, Amon: the chief deity of the period known as the New Kingdom]. The king has sent his messenger to inform the whole land." This was the proclamation of the Pharaoh Ramses II, who ruled Egypt in the 1200s B.C.

The main duty of the priests was to serve the god, whose statue in the inner sanctuary of the temple was treated like a living being. The god's image had to be awakened in the morning, washed and dressed, and offered food and drink. Incense was burned in its honor, and its privacy was strictly guarded. The statue was removed from the temple and carried among the people only on festival days, which took place once or twice a year.

This carving of a kneeling priest was found in the tomb of a high-ranking official.

The priesthood, which was usually hereditary, evolved over time into those priests who served a particular god as a delegate of the king, and those who performed other functions as well. Many priests were also healers or doctors. Lawyers and judges were often members of the priesthood, largely because they were able to read and write the difficult Egyptian language. As a result of the process of mummification, priest-healers had a good understanding of the anatomy of the human body, although they did not completely understand the functions of such organs as the heart and the brain. They treated wounds and performed surgery with a remarkable degree of success and prescribed natural remedies ranging from onions and herbs to castor oil for a variety of ailments. Charms and spells also entered into the treatments administered by the priest-doctors, among whom were women practitioners as well as men.

The God Osiris and Family

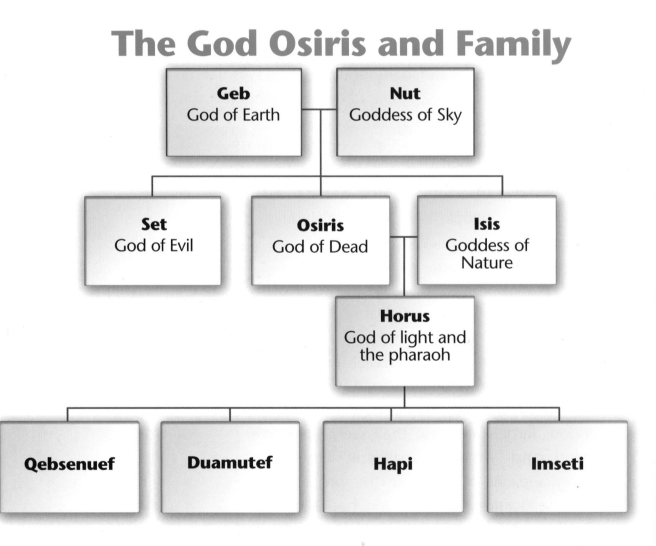

A Look at the Egyptian Gods

In addition to the gods of nature (which included a sky goddess, Nut, and an earth god, Geb), there were gods who oversaw almost every aspect of life: love, nurture, music, and dancing (Hathor); creation and crafts (Ptah); writing (Thoth); truth and justice (Maat); war (Sekhmet); and mummification (Anubis). Most powerful among the legends of the gods was that of Osiris, the god of the dead. Once a beloved king, Osiris was murdered by his jealous brother, Set (or Seth), who tricked him into climbing into a lidded box. Set then slammed the lid shut and cast the box into the Nile, from where it floated out to sea.

Isis, the wife of Osiris, rescued her husband's body from the shore of Asia and brought it back to Egypt. But the wicked Set stole it and cut the corpse of Osiris into fourteen parts, which he scattered all over the land. Magically, Isis retrieved the parts and made the body of Osiris whole again. From that time on, Osiris was the god of the dead. He is often depicted on the walls of the tombs as a mummy wrapped for eternity in bandages of linen. He was also the god of the afterlife. When an Egyptian ruler died, he was said to have "joined" Osiris. Over time, members of other social classes in ancient Egypt were considered to have "become" Osiris after death.

Scribes and Hieroglyphic Writing

No Egyptian could hope to become a priest or a government official without being able to read and write, so an ambitious young boy began at the age of six or seven to study to become a scribe. The need for scribes arose in the early days of farming along the Nile. Government officials had to keep records of the sizes and boundaries of the farmers' fields and of the grain and other crops harvested in order to determine the amount of taxes to be paid.

Scribes helped the government keep track of the size of farmers' lands and determine how much farmers would have to pay in taxes.

They also had to keep accounts of the stored grain in the warehouses. In time, a vast government officialdom would develop in Egypt and the person in charge of the powerful state network would be the king's vizier, his close adviser on domestic matters and, often, in foreign affairs as well.

As farming estates developed, record keeping became even more complicated. There was also the need to write down and copy government rulings and proclamations, religious texts (including the so-called **Book of the Dead**, which sought to guide the deceased through the trials of the afterlife), and works of adventure, song, and poetry.

Many of the scribal schools were located within the precincts of the temples. There the young students began the study of the hieroglyphics, or "sacred carvings," that were the basis of the Egyptian written language.

To the uninitiated, many hieroglyphs appear to be picture signs that stand for the objects they represent or for some other complete word. This is true for some hieroglyphic symbols. There are others, however, that stand for sounds, either singly (like the letters of the Roman alphabet) or for groups of sounds. Still others

A papyrus from the Book of the Dead of Nakht from Thebes is shown here. Nakht was a royal scribe and overseer of the army in the Eighteenth Dynasty.

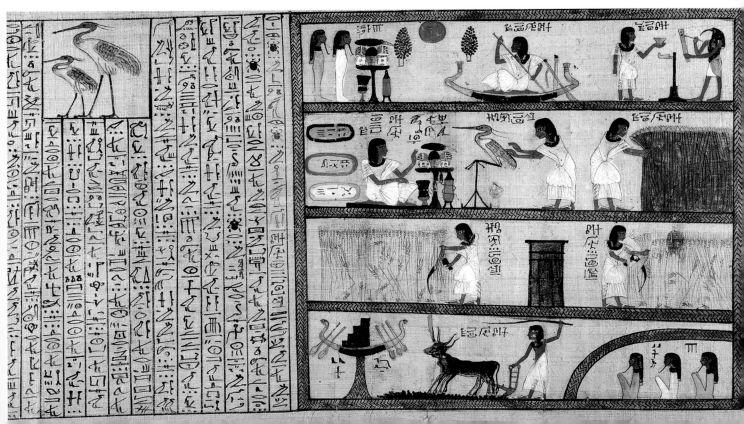

supply vowel sounds to differentiate the meanings of similar-sounding words. All in all, there are about eight hundred hiero-glyphic signs, most of which were in use at any given time. Therefore it is not surprising that memorizing them was so complex and difficult that it was not unusual for the study of writing to take seven or eight years.

The scribe was depicted in Egyptian sculpture as a man sitting cross-legged, his writing scroll stretched across his lap. These long sheets of "writing paper" were time-consuming to produce. They were made from the fibers of the **papyrus** plant, which grew in the Nile marshes. To produce sheets of paper, strips of water-soaked

The discovery of the Rosetta Stone led to a better understanding of Egyptian language and writing.

28

The Rosetta Stone

Hieroglyphic writing is believed to have begun in Egypt around 3000 B.C. The scribes, however, soon found it too slow and laborious to draw the hieroglyphs on papyrus exactly as they appeared on carved monuments and tomb walls. So they developed a kind of cursive writing (as opposed to print) that was known as hieratic. Much later in Egypt's history, around 700 B.C., a simpler, less formal script called demotic writing was developed, and all three systems continued in use. But by about A.D. 500, hieroglyphic writing in all its forms had been forgotten and nobody knew what the carvings on the great ruined temples and other ancient structures meant.

Then in 1799, during their occupation of Egypt, the armies of the French general Napoleon came upon a 4-foot (1.2-meter) high black stone, half buried in the mud near the branch of the Nile that flowed into the Mediterranean Sea near the town of Rosetta. Carved on the stone was an inscription in two languages and three different scripts: Egyptian hieroglyphs, Egyptian demotic writing, and Greek.

Jean François Champollion was a French schoolteacher and scholar of ancient languages, who was intrigued with the centuries-old speculation as to the meaning of the Egyptian hieroglyphics. He attempted, through his knowledge of Greek and **Coptic**, to undertake the decoding of the two Egyptian inscriptions. The text on the stone was a priestly decree honoring King Ptolemy V, who ruled Egypt during the Greek conquest. It had been carved in 196 B.C. By 1822, Champollion had deciphered both forms of Egyptian writing on the Rosetta Stone, opening up a means of reading the language of ancient Egypt and providing an invaluable key to its civilization.

fiber from the pith of the plant were laid atop one another. They were then pounded until they stuck together, dried in the sun, and rubbed smooth with stones or pieces of wood. So student scribes did most of their practicing on smooth chips of limestone, whitewashed wooden boards, or broken pottery, rather than wasting the valuable paper.

Limestone chips, known as **ostraca**, found on the site of the ancient stone workers' village of Deir el-Medina, detail much of its daily life. The scribe's writing equipment consisted of reed brushes and red and black inks. He worked from a wooden palette that had depressions for the inks and slots for the brushes.

Scribes functioned on many levels of Egyptian life. In the villages they wrote letters and documents for the farmers and other members of the illiterate populace. Scribes worked for the government as civil servants. Other scribes produced their own works of literature and became revered as the composers of ballads, poems, and hymns.

No matter what sort of role in society a scribe aspired to, he was considered much better off than those who performed physical labor, such as farmers, craft workers, builders of stone monuments, and warriors. In 2000 B.C., a scribe named Khety strongly advised the youth of Egypt to take up the profession: "It is the greatest of all jobs. See, there is no worker without a boss— except the scribe, who is always his own master. So, if you can learn to write, it will be far better for you than anything else."

Another scribe urged schoolboys, "Become a scribe! Your hands will stay soft. You can wear white clothes. You will be so important that even courtiers will greet you."

Chapter III

KINGS, QUEENS, AND PHARAOHS

Although Egypt is often referred to as the "land of the pharaohs," its kingly rulers were not given that title until the powerful era of the New Kingdom, which began in 1550 B.C. "Pharaoh" is the Greek word for *per-aa,* which means "great house," or palace. Like their titles, the origins and status of those who ruled ancient Egypt changed many times over the course of its three-thousand-year history.

During those millennia, there were periods of great progress and of immense royal power. But these were interspersed with times of instability and decline, which are classified as intermediate periods. In the final centuries of its existence, Egypt was ruled by foreign monarchs, who were mainly of Greek and Roman origin.

The Narmer Palette dates back to the Early Dynastic Period. One side of the palette shows Narmer wearing the crown of Upper Egypt (above) while the other side shows him wearing the crown of Lower Egypt (below).

Early Egyptian Kings

Egyptian royal history dates from about 3100 B.C., when the lands of Upper Egypt (the southern half) and Lower Egypt (the northern half) were united under a single ruler sometimes known as Menes but also frequently referred to as Narmer.

A piece of slate unearthed in 1898, carved with figures that stand out in relief, and known as the Narmer Palette, is presumed to tell the story of the unification of the two parts of the country. Previously, each half of Egypt had been made up of small, independent fiefdoms, each with its own chieftain and local god. It is also possible, according to some Egyptologists, that the country had been united before the reign of Narmer.

In any case, one side of the palette shows Narmer, who is believed to have been the king of Upper Egypt, looming over a kneeling figure and wielding a mace. The figure at his feet appears to be a defeated enemy, presumably an inhabitant of Lower Egypt. Here Narmer wears the pear-shaped white crown of Upper Egypt, but on the other side of the palette he wears the boxy red crown (with a protruding rear shaft and forward-thrusting spiral) that was the symbol of Lower Egypt. So perhaps it is indeed correct that the country was unified before his time.

Nonetheless, rulers after Narmer were portrayed as the "lord of the two lands" and would be shown wearing the double crown—the white crown set into the flat top of the red crown—symbolizing dominion over all of Egypt.

After his conquest Narmer is said to have moved his capital from the southern half of Egypt to a new city in the north in order to consolidate his control over the entire country. This city, near the tip of the delta, became known as Memphis and lay close to the site of the modern Egyptian capital of Cairo.

The dynasties, or hereditary royal families, of Egypt are usually listed as beginning with Narmer, who is considered the first ruler of **Dynasty** 0. The dynasties eventually numbered thirty, according to the most recent findings of the Egyptian department of the Metropolitan Museum of Art in New York City. A king named Aha is usually identified as the first ruler of the First Dynasty.

The era of Dynasty 0 and of the First and Second Dynasties, which extended from 3100 B.C. to 2649 B.C., is classified as the Archaic, or Early Dynastic, Period. This was a time of early development, during which the foundations of a centralized government were laid. Among its major accomplishments was an extended system of canals and basins to irrigate the farming communities along the Nile, for prosperity could be attained only if agriculture flourished and the land was fruitful.

We know about the kings of the Early Dynastic Period from their tombs in burial grounds at Abydos in Upper Egypt, and at Sakkara (also spelled Saqqara) near Memphis, which are called mastabas. The **mastaba** was a rectangular aboveground structure of mud brick, with a flat top and sloping sides. Its name comes from the Arabic word for bench.

At Abydos, the names of the rulers who presumably occupied the tombs are marked with stelae, stone slabs or pillars inscribed with the owners' names. Their bodies, however, may have actually been buried in Sakkara. It is suspected that some of the

Inside a Mastaba

Although the exteriors of the mud brick mastabas were not very impressive, compared with the massive stone pyramids of the rulers that followed those of the first two dynasties, they concealed a surprising amount of wealth. On entering a mastaba one came upon a room that served as a chapel, a place where offerings of food could be made to the deceased king. The major contents of the mastaba lay 40 feet (12 meters) or more underground at the bottom of a narrow shaft, for it was there that the king's burial chamber was located. The burial chamber contained the king's mummy and the rich and ornate possessions he might require in the afterlife.

After the burial chamber was sealed, the shaft leading to it was tightly packed with broken stones, and its entrance from within the mastaba was concealed from view. Like most of the royal burial sites that were to follow, the burial chamber would have been plundered of its treasure. Was it accessed through the blocked shaft? No. Far more cleverly, the Egyptian tomb robbers reached it by digging a long, sloping tunnel, starting at the surface some distance from the mastaba, until they reached their goal—and through which they could make off with the riches within.

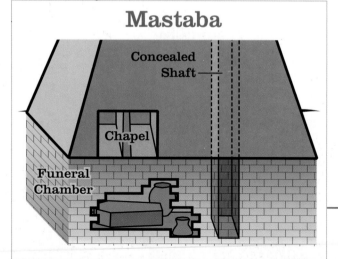

Mastaba

Concealed Shaft

Chapel

Funeral Chamber

mastabas at both places were cenotaphs, empty tombs built to honor rulers whose bodies lay elsewhere.

The Old and Middle Kingdoms

Starting with the rule of the Third Dynasty and lasting through that of the Sixth Dynasty, Egypt experienced a period of great wealth and power referred to as the Old Kingdom (2649 B.C. to 2150 B.C.). The mastaba hardly seemed a fitting burial monument for the Third Dynasty king known as Zoser (or Djoser). So his vizier, or prime minister, Imhotep built him a tomb at Sakkara in advance of his death that became known as the Step Pyramid. It started out as one huge mastaba, with mastabas of decreasing size built on top of it until there were six levels and it reached a height of nearly 200 feet (61 meters). Furthermore, Zoser's Step Pyramid was built of stone rather than mud brick, and so it set the stage for the great pyramids—which were "true," or straight-sided

Zoser's Step Pyramid was designed by his vizier Imhotep and was built during the Third Dynasty. The stone structure was an advanced version of the mud brick mastabas used earlier.

The Great Pyramid

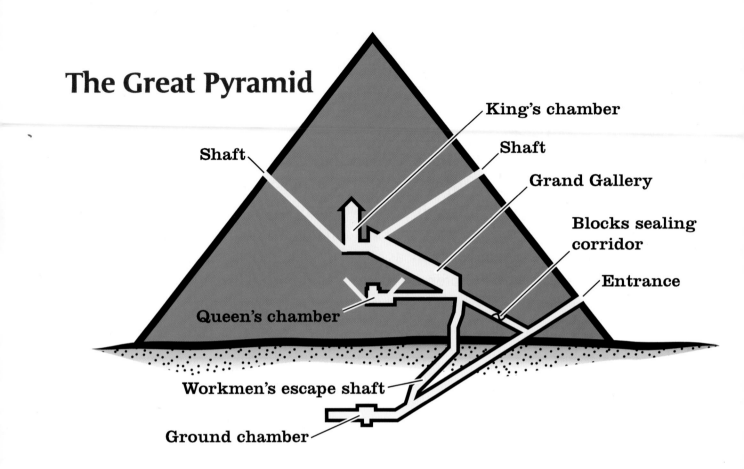

King's chamber

Shaft

Shaft

Grand Gallery

Blocks sealing corridor

Entrance

Queen's chamber

Workmen's escape shaft

Ground chamber

Kings of the 4th Dynasty

Snefru

Khufu

Djedefre

Khafre

Nebka II

Menkaure

Shepseskaf

Thamphthis

pyramids—of the Fourth Dynasty kings. It is believed that these structures were designed to represent the slant of the sun's rays beaming down, by the grace of the sun god Ra, on the king who lay within.

Of the three pyramids built at Giza, just northwest of Memphis, the largest is that of King Khufu (also known by his Greek name, Cheops). Khufu's pyramid is composed of more than 2 million blocks of stone, each weighing about 2.5 tons. The

The Wealth of the Fourth Dynasty

Adjacent to the Great Pyramid of King Khufu at Giza stand two somewhat smaller, but nonetheless huge and imposing, pyramids built for Khufu's successors, King Khafre and King Menkaure. Khufu's tomb, which lay within the pyramid, and the tombs of the other two, which were placed underground, were all rifled of their rich contents. How did the kings of the Fourth Dynasty become so wealthy as to afford these great structures and the treasures placed in their tombs?

The luxuries of the Fourth Dynasty were the result of successful expeditions abroad, through which Egypt acquired materials that could be used for trading as well as for its own use. The Sinai Peninsula had by this time become the site of extensive copper and turquoise mining. To the northeast of Sinai was the land known as Lebanon, which was a source of the cedar logs that were much in demand for strong and beautiful building wood. Other expeditions brought back incense from the coast of what is today Somalia, and ivory, gold, and animal skins from the upper reaches of the Nile deep into Africa.

immense structure is 480 feet (146 meters) tall. When Herodotus visited Egypt in about 450 B.C., he was told that it took twenty years and the labor of 100,000 men to build the Great Pyramid.

With the passing of the Fourth Dynasty of the Old Kingdom, Egypt's era of great pyramid building came to a close. Pyramids continued to be built during the final centuries of the Old Kingdom, and also by the kings of the Middle Kingdom (2030 B.C. to 1640 B.C.), but many were so poorly constructed that they collapsed over time. Altogether the rulers of Egypt left behind some eighty pyramids, of which thirty-six may be considered of major significance. Pyramids that were huge mountains of stone stopped being built, partly because of a decline in Egypt's national prosperity. But the main reason was the realization that, no matter how fortresslike, a pyramid was not a secure place for the burial of a bejeweled mummy and its possessions.

The Glories of the New Kingdom

The beginning of the period known as the New Kingdom (1550 B.C. to 1070 B.C.) signaled a tremendous increase in Egypt's fortunes. The rulers of the Eighteenth and Nineteenth Dynasties left sumptuous tombs cut into the rocky cliffs of the western shore of the Nile at Thebes. It was at this time, too, that the title of pharaoh came into use for the nation's supreme ruler. The word itself meant "great

Queen Hatshepsut was one of the most powerful women to rule ancient Egypt.

house," referring to the palace in which the monarch dwelt.

Outstanding among the rulers of the New Kingdom was a pharaoh who was a woman. Queen Hatshepsut was the daughter of a king, the wife and half-sister of another, and the stepmother and aunt of yet a third. Those male relatives bore the names of Thutmose I, Thutmose II, and Thutmose III. Thutmose I and III were powerful pharaohs, but Hatshepsut is notable as a woman who was also a forceful ruler and who undertook the enrichment of her country through the development of trade and industry.

Her pillared mortuary temple set into the Theban cliffs contains carvings that show scenes from the trading expeditions she sponsored to the land of Punt, probably Somalia in the horn of Africa. Hatshepsut herself was usually portrayed wearing a false beard and men's clothing. But a sculpted head from one of her statues reveals the face of a beautiful woman with an intent gaze.

After Hatshepsut, the Eighteenth Dynasty produced a long line of powerful male pharaohs, many of whom engaged in military campaigns. They lived amid luxury and splendor and built lavish temples and towering monuments to the many gods who had looked favorably upon them. Then along came a pharaoh who was different from all the rest. He was the son and heir of the pharaoh Amenhotep

Akhenaten tried to revolutionize Egypt's religion, eliminating the worship of all of the gods except for one—Aten, the sun.

III and should have been known as Amenhotep IV. But because he believed in the idea of a single god—the sun, which he called Aten—he changed his name to Akhenaten ("pleasing to Aten").

By the time Akhenaten ascended the throne in about 1349 B.C., the Egyptian priesthood had become enormously powerful as a result of the numerous gods its people worshipped. Out of his own religious convictions and to curb the power of the dominant Amun priesthood, Akhenaten closed temples, including those of the chief god, Amun. He then left the royal seat at Thebes and moved the capital of Egypt to a new city located on the Nile about halfway between Thebes and Memphis. He called it Akhetaten ("horizon of the Aten").

The rule of Akhenaten lasted for about thirteen years, during which time he pursued his religious worship of the sun, while neglecting military affairs and allowing the prestige of Egypt to decline. Akhenaten's efforts to guide the country toward the worship of a single god failed completely. But during his rule at Akhetaten a new form of Egyptian art, attributed to the Amarna period, took its place in history.

Akhenaten's successor was a minor king, who may have been his son, brother, or a young son-in-law, and who reverted to the worship of the many gods of Thebes under the reigning cult of the chief god, Amun. He was believed to have been only nine years old when he ascended the throne and eighteen at the time he died, under circumstances that remain mysterious. His fame is not due to his achievements as pharaoh but rather to the fact that his rock-cut

The Amarna Age

After the death of Akhenaten the capital of Egypt was moved back to Thebes, and his city of the sun disk, Akhetaten, fell into ruins. Today it is the site of the Egyptian village of Tell el-Amarna, which has given its name to the art produced there in the 1300s B.C.

Amarna art was a marked departure from the rigid, stylized portrayals of Egyptians that went all the way back to the days of the Old Kingdom. Traditionally, figures were stiff and heads were shown in profile, with eyes drawn as if viewed frontally. It was sometimes difficult for individual faces to be distinguished one from the other.

With the art produced at Akhetaten came a new realism. Akhenaten was a devoted family man, the husband of the beautiful Nefertiti and the father of six daughters. In wall paintings and carvings from the palaces and tombs at Akhenaten's capital, we see informal family scenes showing Akhenaten, his queen, and their children. Often they sit or stand beneath the kindly rays of the sun disk, which descend toward them, each ray ending in a hand that appears to be offering a blessing.

Even more remarkable are the faithful portrayals of Akhenaten's elongated head and deformed body, with its protruding belly and thick thighs, possibly the result of a glandular problem. No other pharaoh would have permitted himself to be so honestly depicted to his people.

tomb, discovered by British Egyptologist Howard Carter in 1922, was almost completely intact. His name was Tutankhamen.

"At first I could see nothing, the hot air escaping from the chamber causing the candle to flicker, but presently, as my eyes grew accustomed to the light, details of the room within emerged slowly from the mist, strange animals, statues, and gold—everywhere the glint of gold."

These were the words of Howard Carter when, on November 26, 1922, he peered through a tiny opening into the first room of the small, four-chambered tomb filled with fanciful furniture made out of ivory, ebony, alabaster, and gilded wood. But the greatest prize was the burial chamber itself, which contained the mummy of Tutankhamen, its face covered with a solid gold mask and its body encased in a nesting series of mummy-shaped coffins, the innermost one made of solid gold.

Unlike almost every one of the rich tombs of Egypt's rulers, that of Tutankhamen had not been robbed of its principal treasures. There was evidence in the disarray of the first chamber that tomb robbers had made a clumsy attempt to make off with some of the smaller articles but had been interrupted. Then, as the tombs of succeeding kings had been dug in the valley, the huts of quarrymen and other workers were erected over the very entrance to the tomb of Tutankhamen, concealing its existence until Carter came upon it.

The Eighteenth Dynasty, with its many achievements, came to a disappointing end shortly after the death of Tutankhamen. It was succeeded by the Nineteenth Dynasty, which was dominated by the sixty-seven-year reign of the pharaoh Ramses II.

In his search for lasting fame and grandeur, Ramses II extended the vast temple complex on the eastern bank of the

Nile at Thebes (known as Karnak). He erected needlelike stone columns, known as **obelisks**, inscribed with his name and his military achievements. Moreover, he erected massive statues in his likeness. He even put his name onto older royal statues to ensure a broad and lasting legacy. But he could not recapture for Egypt

Howard Carter, an Egyptologist, discovered the tomb of Tutankhamen, a pharaoh from the Eighteenth Dynasty.

the vigor it had enjoyed during the reigns of Eighteenth Dynasty kings such as Thutmose III.

Discontent within Egypt and agitation from enemies without the empire began to take their toll. Although Egypt's decline as a great and independent power was gradual, the conditions that would lead it into an unstable Late Dynastic Period and eventually into an era of foreign domination were already in place.

Yet the abiding relationship between the rulers of ancient Egypt and its people was of the utmost significance. From the earliest days the king was recognized as the agent of the gods and the intermediary between the divine world and the human world. He was the upholder of the established order of the universe—as well as the virtues of justice and truth—as personified by the goddess Maat.

The death of an Egyptian monarch demanded a royal burial and entombment in a grand and often sumptuous monument. Properly appointed in such surroundings, his existence in the afterlife and his continuing intercession with the gods on behalf of his subjects would be guaranteed.

In spite of those kings, from time to time, who were self-serving, indifferent, or worse, reverence for the institution of supreme rulership remained and, for the most part, sustained the civilization of ancient Egypt through its millennia.

Ramses II had this
self-glorifying
statue of himself
erected at Karnak.

Chapter IV

BUILDERS IN STONE

Preparations for the construction of the great stone monuments of ancient Egypt involved a great deal of planning. Architects had to determine the most favorable site for each, draw up a design for the project, and calculate the kinds and amounts of material that would be required.

None of their imaginings could have been realized, however, without the labor of those who did the actual building. Ancient Egypt had no iron to make strong hacking and cutting tools, no lifting machinery of any kind, and no wheeled vehicles. Every step of the way, from the quarrying of the stone, its transport to the building site, and the construction itself, had to be achieved through human ingenuity and by the application of sheer physical power.

Constructing the Pyramids

One of the earliest standing monuments, the step pyramid of the Third Dynasty king, Zoser, was constructed of relatively small stones, in imitation of the mud brick that had been used earlier for the royal mastabas. The stones were quarried from local sources. But to build a pyramid that had a much larger base and stood nearly two-and-a-half times taller—such as the Great Pyramid of the Fourth Dynasty king, Khufu—it would have been extremely time- and labor-consuming to use such small units of stone.

For the three huge pyramids at Giza, as well as others of their day, the Egyptians quarried bedrock limestone from the surrounding desert. After hewing the immense blocks of stone from the rock, the work crews trimmed and shaped them with tools of stone, copper, or bronze, and dragged them on sleds to the building site. The granite that was used to line the burial chambers of the pyramids came from much farther afield, the southern quarries that lay near the First Cataract of the Nile. Those stones were transported by boat to Giza on the north-flowing currents of the Nile, where they were transferred to the building site on sleds with wooden runners.

The laborers who constructed the pyramids were not foreign captives or slaves, as has sometimes been believed. They were, for the most part, Nile farmers who were sufficiently idle during the

Workers moved building blocks across the sand on a type of sled.

four-month period of Akhet, when the Nile River was flooding its banks, to devote their time to the construction of a pyramid tomb for their king. Their religion taught them that the proper entombment of the king's mummified body and the existence of his soul in the afterlife assured peace and prosperity for his subjects throughout eternity.

There was no currency in use in Egypt at that time, so the farmers who built the pyramids were paid in food, clothing, and other useful items. The government provided them with meals, lodging, and work tools when they were on the job. Recent excavations at Giza have uncovered the tombs, built with construction debris, of the pyramid work crews. As many as 30,000 workers and their families may have lived on the site at a given time. In addition to the laborers, there were toolmakers, artisans, bakers and brewers, storekeepers, guards, and overseers, as well as scribes and government officials.

As the stone slabs were placed atop one another, by means of either sledges or earthen ramps, the inner rooms were constructed as well. In the Great Pyramid of Khufu, they consisted of sets of passages leading to chambers, including the king's burial chamber, which was later robbed of all its contents.

The outer surfaces of the pyramids were coated with polished white limestone blocks, quarried from the eastern desert across the Nile, for a finish that was smooth and gleaming. But in later times the Muslim rulers of Egypt stripped much of the limestone from the pyramids to build their own palaces and places of worship. The pyramid of Khafre, the second largest at Giza, still has a capping of the original limestone. But most existing surfaces at Giza are of rough-edged blocks that have worn away in places, providing a surface that can be climbed with relative ease.

In ancient times, each of the pyramids at Giza, as well as elsewhere, were surrounded by a complex of smaller pyramids and mastabas to serve as tombs for other members of the royal families. A causeway led from a valley temple at the eastern end to a mortuary temple at the western end, in front of the pyramid. Although most of these surrounding structures have crumbled, the figure of the Great **Sphinx** still stands, almost directly in front of the pyramid of Khafre.

The Great Sphinx

Unlike the pyramids, the mysterious figure with the body of a lion and the head of a man was not built stone by stone. It was carved instead out of a great boulder, a natural outcropping of desert rock. As the rock lay near the causeway to the pyramid of Khafre, sculptors chose to chisel away at it until the body resembled that of a crouching lion and the head that of King Khafre wearing the traditional royal headdress, known as a nemes.

Lion-bodied sphinxes with the heads of humans or animals, such as rams or hawks, are found at other sites in Egypt as well. These fanciful creatures usually represent either powerful rulers or important gods. An impressive avenue of ram-headed sphinxes depicting the god Amun lines one of the entrances to the Temple of Karnak at Thebes.

The sphinx at Giza is 240 feet (73 meters) long and stands 66 feet (20 meters) high. Unfortunately the stone face that was meant to be an image of King Khafre was marred by attempts to destroy its features in relatively recent times.

Egyptian Temples and Obelisks

Temples that served various purposes were built throughout Egypt's long history. The very earliest Egyptian temples were small structures made of mud bricks and reeds. Often the trunks and fronds of palm trees served as columns. The Egyptians soon turned to building their temples out of stone, even the small mortuary temples on the causeways leading to the great pyramids. These boxy structures housed statues or other images of the deceased monarch to which special priests could make offerings, usually in the form of food or drink.

The stone temples that were built to honor the gods were more complex. They were entered through massive gates that

This illustration imagines what the temple at Karnak looked like in ancient times.

led to halls of tall columns. Deep within lay the sanctuary where the statue of the temple god presided.

The most extensive temple of the New Kingdom was Karnak, located on the eastern bank of the Nile at Thebes. It was dedicated to the god Amun, and almost every pharaoh of the Eighteenth and Nineteenth Dynasties tried to add something to it in order to please Amun. As a result, its walls and columns were thick with hieroglyphic inscriptions and carvings in praise of the god who dwelt within the temple.

The builders in stone of the temples of the New Kingdom were called upon to provide details that made their work very different from that of the pyramid builders of the Fourth Dynasty. Crudely finished blocks of stone would not do. The columns that held up the temple roofs, for example, were fashioned to resemble various kinds of Nile vegetation. Some columns represented the palm trees that had been used for support in the earliest temples. Others were carved with the shafts and tops of the columns to look like lotus or papyrus plants.

Other features of the great temples were obelisks, or slender four-sided, free-standing columns cut from single slabs of stone. The four tapering sides of these needlelike shafts were shaped like small pyramids at the top and were sometimes capped with gold to catch the rays of the sun.

The obelisk known as Cleopatra's Needle is not connected to the famous ruler Cleopatra VII. It now stands in Central Park in New York City.

Ancient Egyptian Obelisks

Even more baffling than the building of the pyramids is the question of how the Egyptians cut these brittle shafts of stone from the rock without breaking them, transported them to temples or other sites, and upended them to remain standing.

True, many obelisks broke at one stage or another, but many more were successfully erected.

It is believed that the method used was to chisel long rows of deep holes into the bed of granite from which the obelisk was to be freed. Once the bronze chisels had done their job, stout poles of cedar wood were inserted into the cavities and wetted down until they swelled. Tremendous human force was then applied on the wooden poles to split open the seam of rock.

Today, some of the obelisks that once stood in ancient Egypt may be found in Paris, Rome, and London, and one is in New York City's Central Park, where it is erroneously referred to as Cleopatra's Needle. The Central Park obelisk dates from the fifteenth century B.C., while Egypt's Ptolomaic queen did not come on the scene until the first century B.C.

The Monuments of Ramses II

No pharaoh of ancient Egypt was more demanding of the labors and the skills of his stonecutters than was Ramses II. During his long reign he ordered immense portraits of himself in stone, which appeared throughout the Egyptian empire from the Nile delta in the north to a place called Abu Simbel, near the present Sudan border in the south.

At the Temple of Karnak and the adjacent Temple of Luxor, on the eastern bank of the Nile at Thebes, Ramses erected towering royal images. His statue at the Temple of Karnak shows him wearing the double crown of Egypt. Standing on his immense toes and reaching only to his thighs is a stone figure of one of his wives. Can we assume that her relatively small size is an indication of her very minor importance?

On the western bank of the Nile, Ramses II had a mortuary temple, the Ramesseum, built for himself. The front of the temple was flanked with two immense seated figures, each more than 50 feet (15 meters) tall and weighing 1,000 tons. The forefingers of the statues were one yard, or nearly a meter, long.

The Ramesseum statues eventually broke into fragments. One of them, a giant toppled head, rests to this day in the desert sands at the foot of the temple ruins. But Ramses II provided enough images of himself in stone to survive history.

At Abu Simbel, the farthest south that the builders of Egypt had ever been sent to erect monuments, the pharaoh ordered a great temple dedicated to himself, as a god, and to three other gods: the sun god, Ra; the creator god, Ptah; and the god Amun. A smaller temple at Abu Simbel was built for Ramses's favorite wife, Nefertari, and was dedicated to Hathor, the goddess of love and nurturing.

The façade of the larger temple consisted of four giant seated figures of Ramses, each 60 feet (18 meters) tall, with much smaller figures of his mother, wives, and children scattered at his feet, reaching only to the calves of his legs. The temple was carefully situated so that at certain times of the year its interior would catch the rays of the rising sun. And so it sat for more than three thousand years until the A.D. 1960s, when the Egyptian government found it necessary to increase the size of the dam at Aswan north of Abu Simbel. The dam would create a huge lake that would drown the temple of Ramses II plus the smaller temple dedicated to Nefertari and their children. Was this the end of glory for the great pharaoh?

The Saving of Abu Simbel

Through the fundraising efforts of the United Nations, a tremendous project was undertaken to save the temples at Abu Simbel.

Between 1964 and 1968, at a cost of $40 million, the temples were moved 200 feet (61 meters) above their original site onto an artificial mountain resembling the one from which the temples were carved.

The temples, with all their statuary, were cut up into 1,200 pieces, lifted individually by hoists, and reassembled to resume their original appearance. Not only did they sit well above the waterline of the new lake, but the temple of Ra, fronted by the four great statues of Ramses, was oriented to catch the rays of the rising sun exactly as before.

The survival of Abu Simbel may be seen as a triumph for the ambitious and egotistical Ramses II. It is, more honestly, a tribute to the builders in stone who created the monuments that can still be viewed in Egypt today.

Ramses II had this temple built at Abu Simbel. Four giant stone statues of this pharaoh are seated at the entrance.

Chapter V

QUARRYMEN AND CRAFT WORKERS

With the passing of the era of pyramid building, the ancient Egyptians embarked on a new type of tomb construction. Mainly during the New Kingdom, starting in 1550 B.C., and extending over a period of nearly five centuries, they were to bury their exalted dead in tombs that were cut out of sheer rock.

These tombs were located not in Lower Egypt, where the pyramids stood, but in a region of high, stony cliffs that lay just beyond the fertile Nile shore, on the western bank of the river, at a place called Thebes in Upper Egypt. The stony desert burial grounds came to be known as the Valley of the Kings, the Valley of the Queens, and the Valley of the Nobles.

The Royal Tombs of Thebes

The workers who built, decorated, and furnished the sumptuous tombs of the New Kingdom were among the most skilled in Egypt. They were brought together to live with their families in a village of stone houses that was built in the rocky

Egyptian artisans are shown at work. Many of them are making objects that will
be buried in tombs as part of Egyptian funerary practices.

desert close to where the tombs themselves were excavated. The village is today called Deir el-Medina.

Unlike the mud-brick houses and even the farming estates that comprised other Egyptian villages, which vanished almost without a trace with the passage of time, the stone structures of Deir el-Medina have survived. As a result, we have been able to learn a great deal about the way ordinary Egyptians lived. The village housed as many as seventy families at any one time and was inhabited for more than four hundred years.

Deir el-Medina was unlike other Egyptian villages, however, because of its remote location. Its distance from fertile fields and the life-giving Nile meant that its quarrymen and craft workers—which included carpenters, draftsmen, painters, sculptors, and artisans of many kinds—had to be supplied with food and water, as well as most of their work materials.

The Egyptians divided their thirty-day months into three ten-day weeks of eight working days and two rest days each. Paths, which are still visible, led the inhabitants of the village to the exact site of the tomb that was under construction. There they would camp out in crude stone huts for the eight working days, surveying, cutting the stone for the tomb, and finally plastering and decorating the interior walls.

Their cutting tools were mainly bronze chisels and wooden hammers. For the decoration of the interior walls, the draftsmen, painters, and sculptors often began by drawing grids that indicated the placement of the figures of gods, humans, and animals, scenes from nature, hieroglyphic inscriptions, and whatever else was called for.

The painters' brilliant hues of red and yellow, as well as blue, green, black, and white pigments, were obtained from mineral sources such as ocher, copper, malachite, carbon, and chalk.

Two sculptors
are seen carving
a statue on a
relief found
in a mastaba
from the Old
Kingdom.

Shabtis, the Servants of the Dead

In addition to the numerous crafted objects placed in the tombs for the comfort and pleasure of the deceased, there were miniature figures of servants known as **shabtis** (or shawabtis). Standing in attendance, wrapped like mummies with crossed arms, the doll-like shabtis were made out of painted or carved wood, stone, or pottery, and ranged in size from a few inches to more than a foot tall. They were first discovered in the tombs of the Middle Kingdom (2030 B.C. to 1640 B.C.), with usually only one shabti to a tomb.

In the tombs of the New Kingdom (1550 B.C. to 1070 B.C.), shabtis were much more numerous. In some cases there was one for every day of the year, plus an overseer for each of the year's thirty-six full weeks, bringing the total to four hundred and one. The shabtis were present not only to

wait on the deceased. They were also meant to stand in for the master or mistress in case Osiris, the god of the dead, requested them to perform various duties in the afterlife. As a result, they were also known as answerers. The name comes from the Egyptian verb *usheb*, "to answer."

Sculptors carved the tomb walls so that figures and other decorations stood out in relief. They also made statues of the deceased in miniature or full size. Meanwhile, working usually back in the village, skilled artisans produced tomb objects ranging from exquisite inlaid wooden boxes to utilitarian pottery vessels, from fine jewelry and elegant funerary masks to large items of furniture. They did not fail to provide toilet articles and cosmetics, or sandals for the feet should the deceased desire to venture forth in the afterlife.

The decoration alone of a large tomb was known to take at least two years. But the Egyptian obsession with a suitable burial site replete with every requisite for the afterlife meant that most royal tombs were begun as soon as an Egyptian ruler ascended the throne. The private tombs of wealthy and important Egyptians were also begun long before their owners died.

Crafts, Jewelry, and Cosmetics

Craft workers in ancient Egypt produced many items for the living as well as for the dead. Local materials for everyday tools and household utensils were limited mainly to stone, wood, and pottery, such as the ceramic vessels in which beer and wine were stored.

Baskets for grains, beans, and other dry foods, as well as for clothing and personal items, were woven from palm fibers or reeds, as also were rope, mats, and the sandals that most people wore. Even small tables and stools could be woven from the tall grasses that grew along the Nile.

These goods were distributed in farming villages and market towns along the Nile by merchants who traded everything from salt and dried fish to rolls of papyrus and animal hides to the

Scarabs, or Dung Beetles

Popular among Egyptians of all classes were amulets, or charms, in the form of the **scarab**, a beetle that laid its eggs in a ball of dung, or manure. The scarab then rolled the dung underground so that when the young scarabs hatched from the eggs they could feed on the moist dung.

The Egyptians viewed the idea of life arising from a ball of dung as a symbol of immortality. The god of the rising sun, Khepri, was sometimes portrayed as a large dung beetle pushing the sun, as it rose above the eastern hills of the desert, across the sky. The very name of the god derived from the words "to become," or "to come into existence."

As a result, scarab-shaped rings, pendants, and seals were produced in vast quantities out of materials ranging from clay or stone to semiprecious jewels. The flat underside of the scarab was inscribed with hieroglyphics to protect the wearer or owner of the charm against evil. In some cases, the inscriptions commemorated an important event such as a royal birth or a successful expedition to a foreign land. Scarabs found in Egyptian tombs are often inscribed with texts from the Book of the Dead. Scarab jewelry is still fashionable in many parts of the world today.

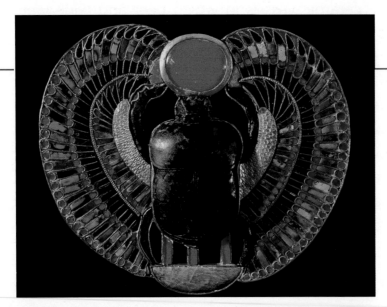

populace. As there was no standard currency in use, most transactions were conducted through barter. Farmers, for example, might offer agricultural products for manufactured items.

Leather obtained from animal hides was usually reserved for such items as drum covers, shields, and thongs for tools and weapons. Sandals made of leather, instead of woven palm leaves or dried reeds, were worn mainly by people of wealth.

To get such luxury materials as gold, which adorned kings and other royalty, Egyptian expeditions ventured into the desert and south to the land called Nubia, which is today the northern Sudan. Turquoise and copper were mined on the eastern shores of the Red Sea, modern Egypt's Sinai Peninsula. But the ancient craft workers also managed to produce handsome, intricate necklaces and other jewelry out of simple materials such as stone, bone, shells, and **faience**. Faience is a blue-glazed pottery that was made into beads for necklaces, and was used as well for plates, cups, and bowls.

From the cosmetics, wigs, and other items of personal grooming found in the tombs of the wealthier Egyptians, we know that craft workers were engaged in producing such items as polished bronze mirrors, pots to hold face creams and perfumes, and brushes to apply facial makeup.

In life, too, women reddened their nails, the palms of their hands, and the soles of their feet with henna, a red-orange dye obtained from the leaves of the henna plant. Both men and women used **kohl**, a grayish-black or greenish-black mineral paste, to darken the eyelids and outline the eyes. More than a fashionable touch, kohl was considered helpful as protection against the fierce light of the sun. Painted statues, funerary masks, and tomb wall decorations almost always attest to the heavy use of kohl among Egyptians of all classes.

A wall painting shows a banquet scene from around 1400 B.C. Wax cones of perfume are visible on the guests' heads.

Tomb paintings of banquets, musical entertainments, and even religious events frequently depict women and even men in finely pleated linen garments wearing cones atop their heads. The cones were made of perfumed wax and were intended to melt slowly as the evening wore on, scenting the faces, shoulders, and arms of the wearers. In life, too, perfume cones were part of the attire of the upper classes.

The Sidelock of Youth

While priests shaved their heads, most Egyptian men wore their hair cut short, and women favored it shoulder length. Both sexes, however, often wore wigs for a fuller and more elaborate effect. Wig makers served the living and the dead alike. Wealthier Egyptians had their wigs made of human hair, designed for women in an intricate arrangement of braided loops, and made fuller with a padding of straw or palm fibers. Less affluent Egyptians wore wigs of animal wool.

A special style existed for young boys, usually under the age of ten. The head would be partially shaved and the remaining hair swept to one side and braided into a fashion known as the sidelock of youth. Boys studying to be scribes are often pictured wearing their hair this way, perhaps as a sign of purity while studying within the walls of the temple. Girls, too, often wore the sidelock of youth.

WARRIORS AND CAPTIVES

Protected by vast deserts on the east and west, by the non-navigable, boulder-strewn Nile cataracts to the south and the Mediterranean Sea to the north, Egyptian civilization was able to develop peaceably for more than a thousand years. If threats developed within the country, such as thievery or banditry, the farmers of the locality dealt with them. Armed with wooden-handled stone clubs or even metal-toothed farming tools, they banded together to subdue their attackers.

Starting during the Old Kingdom, particularly at the time of the pyramid-building kings of the Fourth Dynasty, Egypt sent expeditions into neighboring areas of Asia and Africa in search of copper, cedar wood, ivory, and gold. These expeditions—whether by land or by sea—were accompanied by government troops, foot soldiers armed with leather shields, bows and arrows, throwing sticks to harass the enemy, and metal-tipped spears.

Wooden figures, made around 2000 B.C., show what the Egyptian army looked like during the Middle Kingdom.

The Hyksos Invasion

The invasion of Egypt by foreign hordes began during the years between the Middle Kingdom and the New Kingdom, known as the Second Intermediate Period (1640 B.C. to 1550 B.C.). The part of Egypt that lay in the Nile delta, closest to the Mediterranean Sea, fell under the yoke of Asiatic nomads and raiders who had pushed into the country from the northeast. The Egyptians called these people the Hyksos. Their success in controlling Lower Egypt for a period of about a hundred years was due to their fighting equipment. The Hyksos used not only superior bows and arrows and other weapons, but they had chariots and horses.

From the time of the Asiatic invasions, the ranks of the Egyptian army included mercenaries, or hired soldiers. Among them were the Medjay, skilled archers from Nubia, Egypt's neighbor to the south. During the New Kingdom, the Medjay were sent north to serve in the armies of the pharaohs and also to guard the great temples and other structures of importance.

Starting with the last kings of the Seventeenth Dynasty, the Egyptians began their counterattacks against the Hyksos, whose invasion had left them weakened and humiliated. The mummy of Seqenenre Tao II, who bravely fought the Hyksos, reveals severe wounds to its skull. The gashes were probably the result of hand-to-hand combat with a Hyksos warrior armed with an exceptionally sharp ax blade or spear. Kamose, the last king of the Seventeenth Dynasty, took on the Hyksos, declaring, "I sailed downstream to beat back the Asiatics, with my valiant army going before me like a flame of fire."

Ahmose, the first king of the Eighteenth Dynasty, took the throne in 1550 B.C. Utilizing the methods and materials of warfare they had learned from the invaders, the Egyptians under Ahmose finally drove the Hyksos rulers from the Nile delta. Especially effective was the Egyptian adaptation of the bow the Hyksos warriors had used. It was composed of wood, bone, and animal sinew, and was both stronger and more flexible than the mainly wooden bows the Egyptians had used formerly.

Even after the Hyksos rulers had retreated to their homeland in Asia, the Egyptians pursued them overland into the region of present-day Israel and Syria. Transport by sea was also expanded. Sailing and rowing boats had long plied the Nile for the shipment of goods. The Egyptians now built large seagoing vessels capable of carrying soldiers, chariots, horses, and weapons out onto the Mediterranean Sea, even to the shores of present-day Turkey, Syria, and Israel.

Empire Builders of the New Kingdom

The shores of Asia were sites of empire that the Egyptians were determined to explore further; Nubia at the southern reaches of the Nile was another. Thutmose I, the father of Queen Hatshepsut, led his armies deeper into Nubia than ever before, negotiating the

Chariots and Horses in Egypt

Egypt had no horses until the invasion of the Hyksos. They used cattle or donkeys for transport. Nor did the Egyptians have any wheeled vehicles. The sight of a Hyksos chariot—drawn by two horses, light, fast, and easily maneuvered—created terror in the heart of an Egyptian foot soldier. Each chariot contained two warriors. One warrior drove the chariot while the other, an armed archer, rained arrows on the enemy. Other Hyksos warriors, wielding long spears, ran behind the advancing chariots.

The experience of the Hyksos invasion changed the Egyptian approach to military readiness. The Egyptians adopted the use of the horse-drawn chariot, improved their weaponry, and outfitted their soldiers in bronze armor like that introduced by the Hyksos. Moreover, the pharaohs of the New Kingdom were no longer content to stay within the boundaries of Egypt, making only trading expeditions abroad. They sought to become builders of empire.

The Blue Crown of War

The white crown of Upper Egypt, set atop the red crown of Lower Egypt, had long symbolized the unification of the country in approximately 3100 B.C. Starting with the New Kingdom, in 1550 B.C., a new type of royal headgear, connected with warfare, came into use. It was a close-fitting blue helmet, often covered with gold disks, and was known as the blue crown of war.

Eighteenth Dynasty monarchs, such as Thutmose I and Thutmose III, who led their armies into the field, wore this crown. The blue crown was also worn by kings who stayed at home, as did Tutankhamen, when they presided at religious ceremonies or over affairs of state, for it reflected Egyptian military might. Like other royal headgear, the blue crown was decorated at the brow with a gilded royal cobra, and often with the head of a vulture as well, for those were the symbols of sovereignty.

rocky waters and dangerous currents and shallows of the Nile cataracts.

His infantry advanced south along the rugged shorelines, launching boats laden with heavy weaponry onto the choppy waters or, when that was impossible, carrying them overland. Gold, ivory, monkeys, and other exotic animals were brought back to Egypt, as well as dark-skinned Nubian captives. The prisoners were intended to serve as slaves or servants to the royal family. Some were conscripted as builders of the temples and other monuments glorifying their captors, while others, like the Medjay, were taken into the Egyptian army.

After the relatively peaceful reign of Queen Hatshepsut, who was married to Thutmose II, her successor, Thutmose III, was ready to take Egypt beyond the boundaries that his grandfather had carved out. He penetrated deeper into Asia, seeking to overcome another Asian people, the Mitanni, whose empire extended from the coast of Syria all the way to the Tigris River in present-day Iraq. Thutmose III fought a famous battle with a vassal army of the Mitanni at Megiddo (today, northern Israel). After a siege of seven months, Thutmose III declared a great victory, which he celebrated with lion and elephant hunts in the territory he claimed to have conquered. Animal hunts as well as human conquests became the twin symbols of the pharaoh's power.

Stone carvings, engravings on tomb ornaments, and paintings on tomb walls show us many examples of warrior kings wielding spears at ferocious beasts or racing in pursuit of them in their chariots. Even young Tutankhamen is depicted—on one of his painted wooden tomb chests—at the helm of a war chariot, drawing his bow in the direction of fleeing Syrians. Although he lived in the shadow of his powerful predecessors, he is believed to have sent warriors abroad on two foreign campaigns.

Tutankhamen is shown in this painting fighting the Syrians. The horse and chariot changed Egyptian warfare.

Ramses II and the Hittites

Egypt's last attempt to secure a completely stable empire in Asia came at the hand of Ramses II, the most prominent pharaoh of the Nineteenth Dynasty. During the 1200s B.C., Ramses fought the Hittites, a powerful people whose empire was based in present-day Turkey. The armies of the two superpowers met at a place called Kadesh, in Syria. Although Ramses claimed a great victory and had inscriptions to that effect carved on many of his monuments, the outcome of the battle remained in doubt.

Ramses II added a Hittite princess to his royal household as one of his wives. But he could not hold the territory and, through a peace treaty with the Hittite ruler, retained control of only that portion of the Hittite kingdom that lay closest to Egypt on the Syrian shore.

The plight of the Egyptian warriors fighting under Ramses II in fierce battles with the Hittites can only be imagined. The Egyptian soldiers were clad in kilts and sandals. Many went barefoot. Aside from their shields made of leather or bronze, the archers had no protection. Other Egyptian foot soldiers were engaged in hand-to-hand grappling with crude knives and spears. While arrows and blunt metal weapons might not have caused immediate deaths, they inflicted horrible wounds that resulted in slow and painful dying.

A wall painting offers a glimpse into the lives of Egyptian soldiers. At the top, recruits are shown listening to an officer. In the middle, the recruits are waiting to be given orders. At the bottom, recruits receive haircuts.

After the death of Ramses II, at close to the age of ninety, the Nineteenth Dynasty pharaohs appeared to have little taste for ever-widening conquest. Gradually the tide of warfare turned the opposite way, and Egypt became the recipient of foreign invasions.

The Nineteenth and Twentieth Dynasties were a time of population movements, due in part to climate changes and crop failures. Libyans from across the western desert, once taken captive by the armies of Egypt, entered the country along with the Sea Peoples. The latter were members of a displaced population from the Balkans and the Black Sea region of Europe.

Nubians pushed northward from the lands along the Nile cataracts that Egypt had taken from them, and actually reached the Nile delta, where they ruled for a time. In Syria, Assyrian peoples conquered the Hittites, from whom they had learned how to smelt iron, which made sharper and more durable war weapons than the bronze of the Egyptians. They, too, invaded Egypt, reaching at one point as far south as Thebes. Little by little the mighty dynasties of Egypt wound down, with the Thirtieth Dynasty coming to an end in 343 B.C.

In 332 B.C. the country, which had been under Persian control for two periods totaling more than a hundred years, was conquered by the Macedonian (Greek) king Alexander the Great, who made it part of his empire. With Alexander's death in 323 B.C., Egypt was seized by one of Alexander's generals, Ptolemy.

Ptolemy founded a line of rulers that remained in power for three hundred years. Ptolemy V, who was honored by the Egyptian priesthood in an inscription on the Rosetta Stone in 196 B.C., was one of his descendants. Best known, however, of the Ptolomaic rulers of Egypt was the young queen Cleopatra VII, who reigned during the first century B.C.

Cleopatra first shared the throne with her younger brother Ptolemy XIII and, after his death, with an even younger brother, Ptolemy XIV, whom she later had put to death. Her attempts to expand Egypt's dominions abroad involved personal relationships with two important figures of ancient Rome—Julius Caesar and Mark Antony. Neither one of these efforts was successful. In 30 B.C., following a naval battle in which Rome was victorious, Cleopatra was driven to suicide and Egypt became a Roman province.

Egypt remained under Roman rule well into the Christian era. After the rise of Islam in the A.D. 600s, it gradually became a primarily Muslim nation. Modern Egypt has carefully preserved its ancient past and has shared its heritage with the world of today.

Cleopatra VII ruled Egypt during the final years of the Ptolomaic Period.

Chapter VII

MUMMY MAKERS

"O flesh of the king, do not decay, do not rot, do not smell unpleasant!" This was the plea of the mummy makers of ancient Egypt as they set about the work of trying to preserve the body of a deceased ruler for eternity.

Why the Egyptians Made Mummies

The Egyptians' idea of drying out the body soon after death in order to keep it from decaying arose from their observation of natural phenomena. We can say that nature, in Egypt, was the first mummy maker. For it was the practice of the very early Nile farmers to bury their dead in the hot, dry sands of the red land—the desert that lay just beyond the fringe of Nile-watered black land on which they grew their crops.

Early burial sites were small, shallow holes into which the unclothed body was placed in a crouched position, knees drawn up to the chest. The families of the departed, believing that the spirit would live on, included small amounts of food, such as dried grains and beans and water in an assortment of clay pots. They might also place in the desert grave a man's favorite flint knife, a woman's shell necklace, a child's plaything.

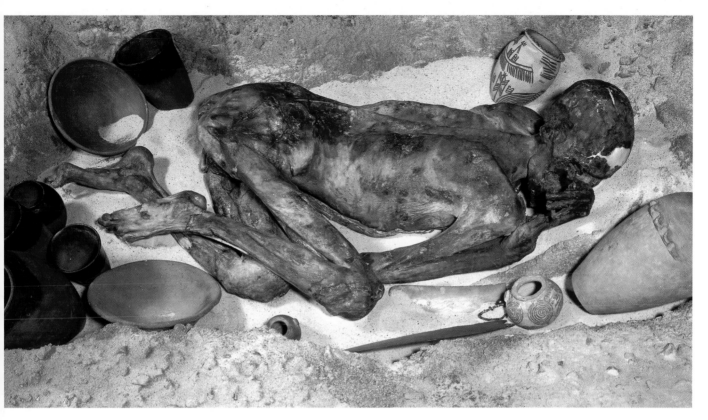

The gravesite was covered with sand and an arrangement of rocks to prevent jackals or other wild animals from preying on the flesh of the deceased. Only on rare occasions did humans disturb the desert gravesites. But when they did, they found to their amazement that, despite the passage of time, the body looked remarkably lifelike. True, it had become dry and leathery due to the natural absorption of moisture by the surrounding sand. Even the internal organs had dried out, preventing decay from within. But faces were still recognizable, hair and nails were intact, and even eyelashes were detectable.

Fortunately, examples of mummies made by nature from as early as 3500 B.C., before the unification of Egypt and the advent of its earliest royal dynasties, have been preserved, the most notable of them being on view in London's British Museum.

A body discovered in an early Egyptian grave was found to have been mummified naturally, through burial in the hot, dry sand. Objects such as clay pots were buried with the body.

The Ka and the Ba

The spirit of the deceased, among the ancient Egyptians, was thought to take two forms. The **ka** was the life force, the spirit of the dead that was thought to live on forever. It was the twin or double for whom the earliest Nile dwellers left food and water in the desert graves and, later, provisions of many kinds placed in the closed tombs.

The **ba** was another form of the spirit of the deceased. It was believed to be the dead person's memory, its consciousness, and its personality. Unlike the ka, which remained in the tomb, the ba had the magic power to leave, passing through walls of stone or passages of crushed rock. It was depicted as a small bird with the head of a human, visiting the world by day and returning to the tomb at night, often bearing a lighted candle.

As Egypt developed into a united land ruled by rich and powerful monarchs, professional mummy makers became an important segment of society. The purpose of making a mummy of the king was to have an exact image of the deceased as a means of ensuring that the ka would continue to exist. In the event that the mummy deteriorated—as many of the early efforts of the mummy makers did—statues of the deceased were also placed in the tombs.

Preserving the Body for Eternity

The efforts of the first mummy makers ended in failure because they had attempted to dry the body without removing the internal organs. They went about correcting their mistake. It may have seemed highly irreverent to slash open the body of a royal person with a sharpened stone knife or a cutting tool of copper or bronze. But if the moist internal organs were not removed, the body cavity could not be dried out and the entire mummy would rot from within.

The organs that the Egyptians removed were the liver, lungs, stomach, and intestines. As these, too, were part of the deceased monarch they were dried separately and each was placed in one of four vessels known as **canopic jars** to rest in the tomb with the mummy. The canopic jars took their name from the city of Canopus in the delta region of northern Egypt, where Osiris, the god of the dead, was worshipped in the form of a vase with a human head. During the Middle Kingdom the jars, which were made of wood, pottery, or stone, had stoppers representing human heads. But in the New Kingdom, the jars were differentiated as to their contents and their stoppers.

The Egyptians did not as a rule remove the kidneys. The heart might be removed and dried and then either put back in the

Painted wooden vessels, known as canopic jars, bear the likenesses of the four sons of Horus (left to right): Hapi, Duamutef, Qebsenuef, and Imseti.

The Four Sons of Horus

Horus was the son of Isis and Osiris. After the murder of Osiris by his wicked brother Set, Horus grew up and defeated Set, but he was said to have lost his left eye in the fierce encounter. As a result, the god Horus was depicted as having the body of a man, the head of a falcon, and a single eye with a tear forming at its base. The eye of Horus was a powerful symbol that often appeared on coffins and on tomb walls to enable the dead to "see again."

The four sons of Horus became the keepers of the dried internal organs of a royal mummy. Duamutef, who had the head of a jackal, capped the jar containing the stomach. The falcon-headed Qebsenuef looked after the intestines. The baboon-headed Hapi oversaw the lungs. And Imseti, who had a human head, was in charge of the liver.

body or placed elsewhere in the coffin. If it was not returned to the body, a carved stone scarab inscribed with prayers was sometimes inserted in its place.

The brain was seldom removed in Old Kingdom and Middle Kingdom burials. But starting with the New Kingdom, the mummy makers removed the pulpy mass from the cranium by breaking through the top of the nasal cavity into the skull with a sharp instrument. The brain tissue was then probably stirred around until it was almost liquid and could be drained out through the nostrils by turning the body upside down.

To completely dry out the body, as well as the organs that had been removed, the Egyptians coated them with **natron**, a powdery white salt that was found in the oases of the western desert. As reported to Herodotus, it took thirty-five to forty days for the moisture of an entire body to be absorbed by the salt. During that time, the body lay on a slanted board with a channel at one end through which the remaining water dripped.

The mummy makers were scorned for their work, because the odor of a natron-encrusted body, drying slowly in the hot Egyptian sun under a roof of reeds, was highly unpleasant. Yet their trade, which was handed down from father to son, was much in demand. As Egypt became increasingly prosperous, especially during the New Kingdom, more and more people who were neither pharaohs nor priests, nobles nor owners of estates, wanted to be mummified and buried in their own private tombs.

The preparation of a royal mummy could take as much as seventy days. After the natron was washed away, the body was dried

A papyrus, part of a copy of the Book of the Dead from the Nineteenth Dynasty, shows the embalming process in the making of a mummy.

Making a Mummy

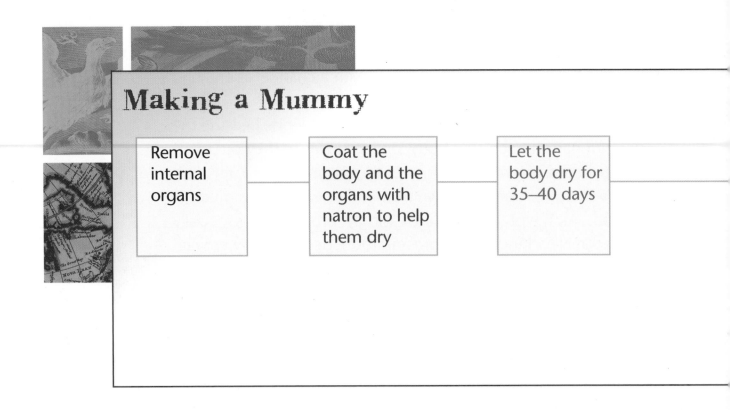

Remove internal organs	Coat the body and the organs with natron to help them dry	Let the body dry for 35–40 days

and its cavities were packed with sweet smelling spices and herbs. Oils and gums were rubbed into the now darkened and leathery flesh, and the entire mummy was wrapped in layers of linen bandages. Between the layers, which might add up to as many as twenty, were placed charms such as scarabs and replicas of the powerful eye of Horus.

The mummy itself was adorned with precious jewelry in the form of necklaces, collars, bracelets, and rings. When the mummy of Tutankhamen was discovered, it was found to have sandals of solid gold on its feet and each toe was encased in a golden sheath.

The bandaged mummy was coated with warm melted resin that hardened to a shellaclike finish that would keep out moisture forever. The mummy was then ready to be fitted with a mask, which might

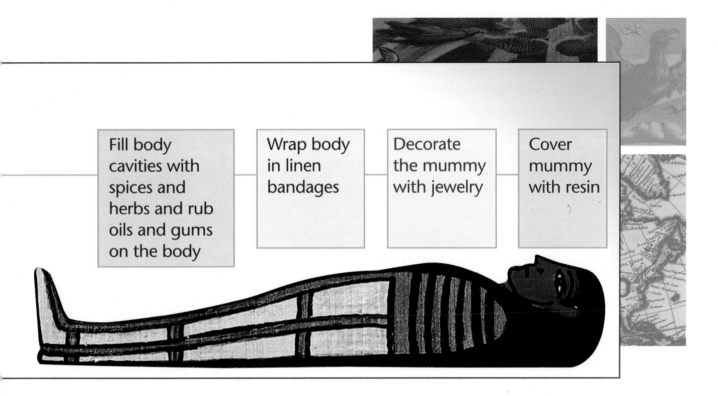

| Fill body cavities with spices and herbs and rub oils and gums on the body | Wrap body in linen bandages | Decorate the mummy with jewelry | Cover mummy with resin |

be richly bejeweled, such as the solid-gold mask of Tutankhamen. Last, the royal mummy was placed in a nest of coffins, often contoured to resemble the shape of the human body, and then encased in a larger cratelike coffin of gilded wood or stone.

The mummy makers of ancient Egypt had their own god, Anubis, who had the body of a man and the head of a jackal. Mummy makers are pictured on tomb walls and in religious texts wearing jackal-headed masks as they perform their duties.

Ancient Egyptian Funeral Processions

Funerals of royalty or other important persons, especially during the New Kingdom, were events that drew enormous crowds. The inhabitants of Thebes, who lived on the eastern bank of the Nile, joined the throngs that gathered there for the burial of major figures from the ranks of the nobility, the priest-hood, or the wealthy citizenry, who aspired to mummification and burial in a private or family tomb.

Crossing from the city of the living to the city of the dead on the western bank of the river required a flotilla of small boats. The empty coffin, or coffins, for the deceased were transported on a wooden sled pulled by oxen that was placed on a boat. On reaching the other side, with its background of grim, stony cliffs, the coffin was taken to the place of mummification, where the prepared body lay in wait.

A large procession of servants and mourners followed the body in its coffin to the tomb site. Everything from large pieces of furniture to clothing and toilet articles, food and drink, hunting gear, and small board games and other pastimes were delivered to the tomb for the comfort and diversion of the deceased in the afterlife.

An Egyptian board game known as senet was so popular with the living that it was unthinkable to omit it from the tombs of the dead. Senet was played with thrown sticks that signaled the movement of pieces around the board, and the very object of the game was to pass successfully into the afterlife.

Wailing, throwing dust on their hair and garments, and beating their heads and chests, the mourners—many of them women who were hired for this purpose—followed the procession to the

entrance to the tomb. There a final ceremony, known as the Opening of the Mouth, took place. Its purpose was to give the mummy
of the deceased its senses back, allowing it to breathe, speak, eat,
see, hear, and move about as formerly, in its life after death.

A wall painting
shows a funeral
procession.
Servants carry
furniture and
other objects to be
buried along with
the deceased.

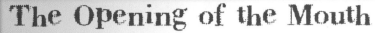

The Opening of the Mouth

At the entrance to the tomb the mummy in its coffin was strapped to a board and made to stand upright. If the arrangement was too clumsy, the mummy was temporarily removed from the coffin. As depicted in paintings on tomb walls, the mummy was supported by a priest wearing the jackal head of the god Anubis, while two other priests touched its mouth, eyes, and ears with a wandlike instrument that had a spur at the tip. A fourth priest, dressed in the traditional leopard skin of Egypt's top-ranking clergy, looked on while the ritual took place.

The Opening of the Mouth ceremony symbolically gave the mummy the ability to share in the funeral banquet. It was also considered to be a test of how well the mummy makers had done their work. Having produced a mummy capable of being a vessel for the ongoing existence of the ka was the moment they had aimed for. Their success assured an afterlife for the deceased.

Chapter VIII

LEGACY
OF
ANCIENT
EGYPT

In examining the history of ancient Egypt, we look back on the lives of people of many social classes. And we realize that the very structure of Egyptian society resembles a pyramid.

The base of the societal pyramid is vast, for it includes the farmers and other providers of food, clothing, shelter, and similar basic needs. Among the army of workers at the bottom are those who built the pyramids, temples, and rock-cut tombs that memorialize and illuminate the Egyptian past.

As the pyramid begins to taper, we come upon lower and then higher orders of craftspeople and artisans, merchants and scribes, overseers and officials, priests, governors, generals, and viziers. Finally, at the very top, are the nobility and the royal rulers.

The division of society into different social classes, or stratification, appears to have worked well for thousands of years. It is one aspect of the Egyptian high regard for order in the structure of society and orderliness in its workings—elements that lie at the core of the Egyptian legacy.

We see order reflected again in the assignment of the Egyptian gods to their various duties. True, other ancient peoples have had similar pantheons. Egypt, however, is notable for the supremacy accorded to the goddess Maat. Truth, fairness, and justice are her hallmarks. Her very name comes from the Egyptian word for order and balance in the universe. The opposite of these virtues, as seen by the Egyptians, were chaos and evil, abominations that they regarded as threats to their very existence.

Harmony in the workings of society is another legacy of ancient Egypt. Each social stratum appears to have functioned compatibly with the other social and professional classes of the time, to the point of showing mutual concern and respect. The example for this regard for others came, ideally, from the pinnacle of the pyramid, from a supreme ruler who would also be fully accountable to his or her people.

Royal accountability among the Egyptians involved an administrative efficiency that reached into every village along the Nile. It ranged from crop irrigation to massive building projects, from the maintenance of local law and order to far-flung trade and military operations. While there were the inevitable self-serving rulers and governmental breakdowns, the goal of royal responsibility remains a major feature of the ancient Egyptian legacy.

While the existence of a stratified social structure and the obsession with order might imply cultural rigidity, another aspect of the Egyptian legacy is creativity. We see it expressed in the architecture, the arts and decoration, and the richly imaginative crafts and jewelry of this ancient people.

The pursuit of beauty in the visual arts is not the only expression of creativity among the Egyptians. We see it, too, in their love of learning, their respect for education, and in their regard for the transmission of knowledge from one generation to the next.

On a more personal note, the ancient Egyptians have left us a deep reverence for family life, as reflected in their attitudes toward the institutions of marriage and the home, especially toward women and children.

The philosophy and beliefs, behavior and achievements of the ancient Egyptians have been preserved for us through their preoccupation with the afterlife and with the preparations they made to ensure its existence. It is largely through the memorials they created to deny death that we are able to know their past and, as a result, to examine and appreciate their rich legacy.

Time Line

**All dates are approximate and based on information from the Metropolitan Museum of Art.

EARLY DYNASTIC PERIOD
3100–2649 B.C.
DYNASTIES 0-2

OLD KINGDOM PERIOD
2649–2150 B.C.
DYNASTIES 3-6

Zoser (Djoser), a prominent Third Dynasty king, has the Step Pyramid built.

Khafre, a son of Khufu, is ruler and has the second largest pyramid at Giza built.

3100 -2649 B.C.   **2630-2611** B.C.   **2551-2528** B.C.   **2520-2494** B.C.

Narmer is the ruler of Dynasty 0 and Aha is the king of the First Dynasty.

Khufu, the most powerful king of the Fourth Dynasty, builds the largest pyramid at Giza to serve as his tomb.

FIRST
INTERMEDIATE
PERIOD
2150–2030 B.C.
DYNASTIES 8-MID 11
(*NO 7)

MIDDLE KINGDOM
2030–1640 B.C.
DYNASTY MID-11–13

SECOND
INTERMEDIATE
PERIOD
1640–1540 B.C.
DYNASTIES 14–17

NEW KINGDOM
1550–1070 B.C.
DYNASTIES 18–20

1665 B.C. Hyksos invasions begin.

Kamose, the last ruler of the Seventeenth Dynasty, begins campaign to expel the Hyksos.

2490–2472 B.C. 2030–1640 B.C. ca. 1560 B.C. 1552–1550 B.C. 1550–1525 B.C.

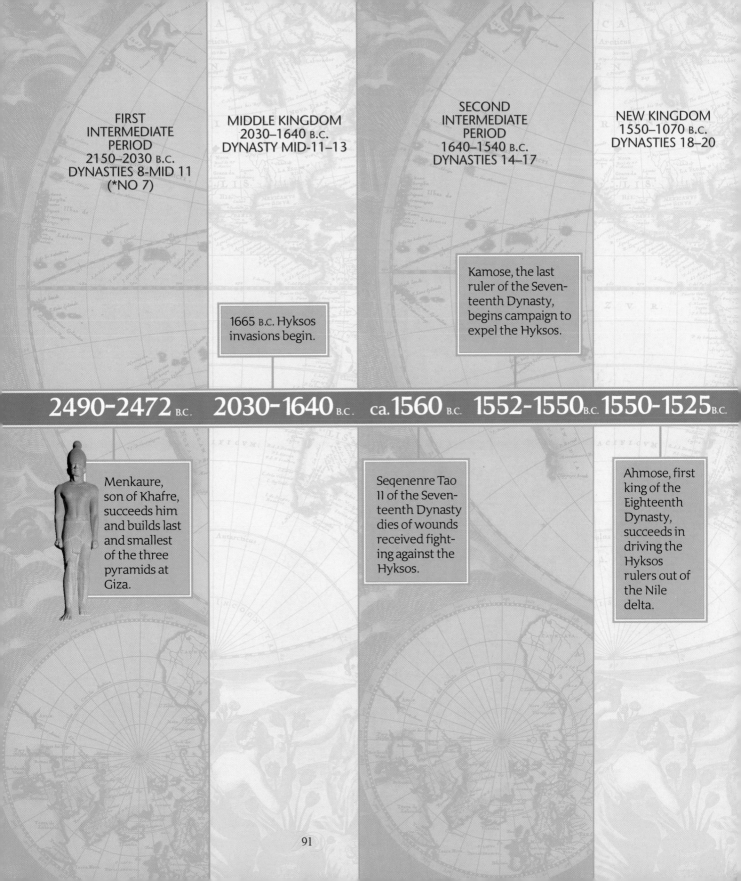

Menkaure, son of Khafre, succeeds him and builds last and smallest of the three pyramids at Giza.

Seqenenre Tao II of the Seventeenth Dynasty dies of wounds received fighting against the Hyksos.

Ahmose, first king of the Eighteenth Dynasty, succeeds in driving the Hyksos rulers out of the Nile delta.

NEW KINGDOM
1550–1070 B.C.
DYNASTIES 18–20
(continued)

Thutmose II, son
of Thutmose I and
husband and half–
brother to Queen
Hatshepsut, is
ruler.

Thutmose III, son of Thutmose II,
first takes the throne as a child,
but his aunt, Queen Hatshepsut,
daughter of Thutmose I, rules
for many years as regent for her
nephew and later in her own
right. After the death of
Hatshepsut, Thutmose III leads
Egypt on military expeditions
to Asia.

1504-1492 B.C.   **1492-1479** B.C.   **1479-1458** B.C.   **1479-1425** B.C.

Thutmose I,
a powerful
monarch of the
Eighteenth
Dynasty, is the
first to be
buried in the
Valley of the
Kings at
Thebes.

Queen
Hatshepsut is
the primary
ruler of Egypt
for nearly
twenty years.

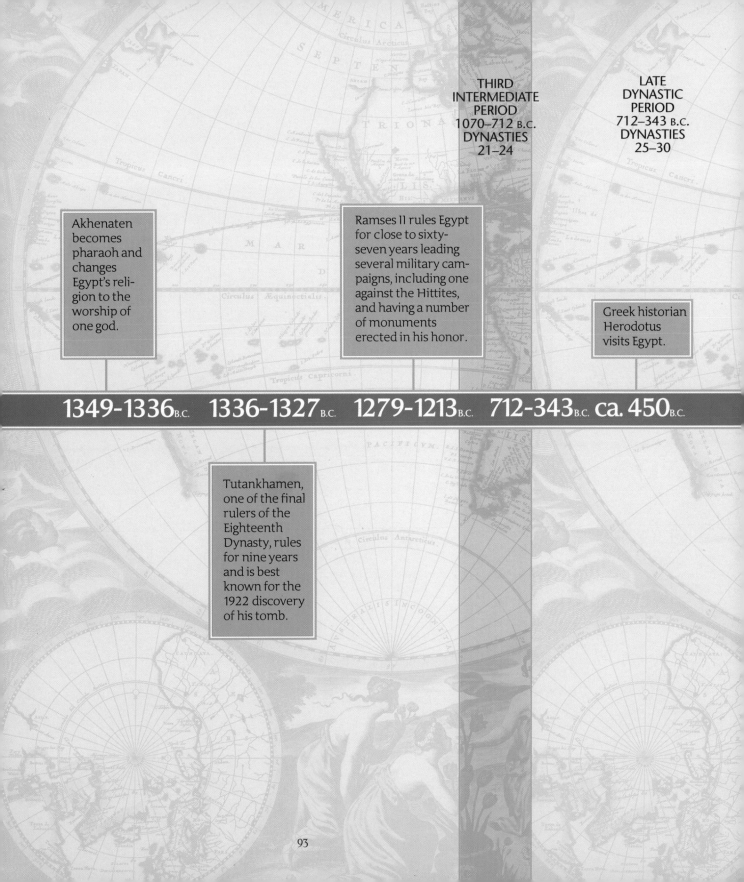

THIRD
INTERMEDIATE
PERIOD
1070–712 B.C.
DYNASTIES
21–24

LATE
DYNASTIC
PERIOD
712–343 B.C.
DYNASTIES
25–30

Akhenaten becomes pharaoh and changes Egypt's religion to the worship of one god.

Ramses II rules Egypt for close to sixty-seven years leading several military campaigns, including one against the Hittites, and having a number of monuments erected in his honor.

Greek historian Herodotus visits Egypt.

1349-1336 B.C.   **1336-1327** B.C.   **1279-1213** B.C.   **712-343** B.C.   **ca. 450** B.C.

Tutankhamen, one of the final rulers of the Eighteenth Dynasty, rules for nine years and is best known for the 1922 discovery of his tomb.

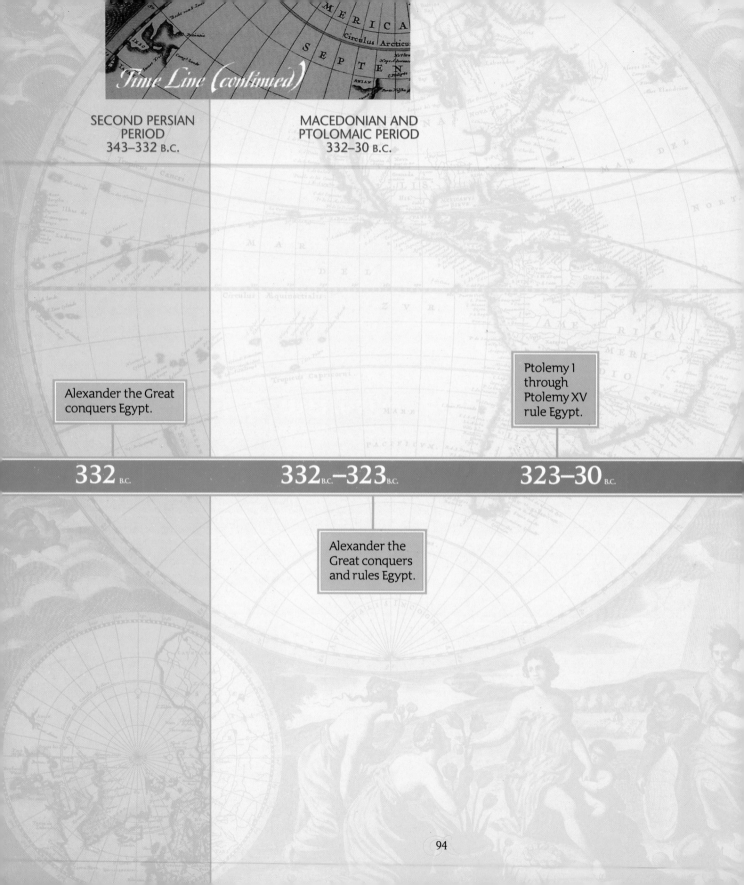

SECOND PERSIAN
PERIOD
343–332 B.C.

MACEDONIAN AND
PTOLOMAIC PERIOD
332–30 B.C.

Alexander the Great
conquers Egypt.

Ptolemy 1
through
Ptolemy XV
rule Egypt.

332 B.C.

332 B.C.–323 B.C.

323–30 B.C.

Alexander the
Great conquers
and rules Egypt.

94

Cleopatra VII assumes the throne as a co-ruler with her brother, Ptolemy XIII. Later, she becomes ruler.

196 B.C.   **51** B.C. **–30** B.C.   **30** B.C. **– 14** A.D.

The Rosetta Stone is carved during the reign of Ptolemy V.

Augustus, the first emperor of Rome, rules Egypt.

Aha

He was the first king of the First Dynasty. His tomb complex at Abydos in Upper Egypt contained the skeletons of young men believed to have been sacrificed for the royal burial, as well as the remains of seven or more young lions. The practice of sacrificing humans to serve in the king's afterlife ceased after the earliest dynasties.

Ahmose

He was the first king of the Eighteenth Dynasty, drove the Asiatic invaders known as the Hyksos out of northern Egypt and regained Nubian lands in the south. His victories inaugurated the period of ancient Egyptian supremacy known as the New Kingdom.

Akhenaten

He was the son of the Eighteenth Dynasty pharaoh Amenhotep III, and was to have ruled as Amenhotep IV. However, he rejected the worship of many gods and particularly that of the chief god, Amun, which was supported by a powerful priesthood. Renaming himself Akhenaten, after the Aten or sun disk, to be worshipped as a single god, he moved his capital to a new site called Akhetaten, or horizon of the Aten. Akhenaten's rule lasted for thirteen years.

Alexander the Great

He was the famed Macedonian (Greek) general, conquered Egypt in 332 B.C., wresting it from the Persian kings of the Second Persian Period. On Alexander's death, in 323 B.C., a succession of rulers descended from his general Ptolemy were in power for nearly three hundred years.

Cleopatra VII

She was the Greek queen of the Ptolemaic line who ruled Egypt in the First Century B.C. Her death by suicide in 30 B.C. signaled the end of Greek sovereignty and opened the era of Roman rule in Egypt.

Hatshepsut

She was a reigning monarch of Egypt during the Eighteenth Dynasty. She was the daughter of Thutmose I and the aunt and stepmother of Thutmose III. She was also the wife and half sister of Thutmose II. During her twenty-year rule she built a magnificent mortuary temple, among other projects, and sent trading expeditions to Punt, or Somalia, in the horn of Africa.

Imhotep

He was the vizier and royal architect of King Zoser of the Old Kingdom's Third Dynasty. He designed the Step Pyramid at Sakkara as a burial structure for the king. Built of stone and six layers high, the Step Pyramid represents a link between the mud brick mastaba and the "true," or straight-sided, pyramids that were to follow.

Kamose

He was the last king of the Seventeenth Dynasty. He came to the throne at the end of the Second Intermediate Period, a time of weakened central government due to the invasions of the Hyksos in the north and the Nubians in the south. His campaigns against the Hyksos paved the way for his successor, Ahmose, who drove them out of Egypt.

Khafre

He was the son of Khufu, the Fourth Dynasty king whose pyramid dominates the three large structures at Giza. The pyramid of Khafre is only the second largest, but it is built on higher ground, making it appear equal or taller from certain distances. It is fronted by the Great Sphinx, which is said to bear the facial features of Khafre.

Khufu

He was the second king of the Fourth Dynasty. He ordered his funerary structure, the Great Pyramid of Giza, to be built soon after he ascended the throne. Work on this largest of all Egyptian pyramids continued almost throughout Khufu's twenty-three-year reign. The burial chamber was located within the pyramid rather than beneath it. Despite elaborate precautions to seal the king's mummy and his treasures within walls of stone, the tomb chamber was eventually robbed of all its contents.

Menes

He is the name of the legendary first king of a unified Egypt. His name is sometimes associated with that of Narmer. Other sources associate Menes with Aha. Whether Menes was the first ruler of Dynasty 0 or the founder of the First Dynasty is not historically clear.

Menkaure

He was the son of the Fourth Dynasty king, Khafre, and the grandson of King Khufu. His pyramid at Giza is the smallest of the three great structures. It was, however, built with proportionately more of the costly granite, which had to be transported from distant southern quarries, than the other two. Pyramids built later not only were smaller but were constructed with less care and attention to detail.

Narmer

He is considered to have been the first ruler of Dynasty 0, although it is believed that Upper and Lower Egypt may have been united before his time and before the events portrayed on the Narmer Palette.

Nefertari

She was the "great royal wife" of the Nineteenth Dynasty pharaoh Ramses II. Her parentage is unknown, but her status was superior to that of his many other wives and she accompanied Ramses as his queen on occasions of state. Her name and likeness appear on many monuments built by Ramses II, and she is recalled especially upon viewing the temple he built for her at Abu Simbel, adjacent to his own larger temple. Nefertari also received a royal burial in a richly decorated tomb in the Valley of the Queens.

Nefertiti

She was the wife of the Eighteenth Dynasty pharaoh Akhenaten, who rejected the traditional religion of Egypt, dominated by the Amun priesthood. At Akhetaten, the city of the sun god, Aten, Nefertiti is frequently portrayed with her husband, making offerings to the sun disk, its rays beaming down upon both of them and, often, on their growing family. Akhenaten and Nefertiti had six children, all daughters. If Tutankhamen were the son of Akhenaten, he would have been the offspring of the pharaoh and a minor wife. Nefertiti's distinctive beauty is preserved in the famous painted limestone head that is on view at the Berlin Museum.

Ptolemy V

He was one of fifteen kings of Greek origin named Ptolemy who ruled Egypt from 323 B.C. to 30 B.C. He was descended from a general of Alexander the Great, who founded the Ptolemaic dynasty. Ptolemy V is remembered for the inscription on the Rosetta Stone, conferring honors on him in 196 B.C. The carvings were in two versions of the Egyptian language and in classical Greek. Reading the inscription in Greek led to the deciphering of the Egyptian language.

Ramses 11

He was a prominent pharaoh of the Nineteenth Dynasty and the last of the powerful rulers of the New Kingdom. He reigned for close to sixty-seven years, undertook a vast building program, and left monuments to himself all over Egypt. He also engaged in military campaigns abroad, claiming a huge victory over the Hittites at the battle of Kadesh in present-day Syria. Ramses II had numerous wives in addition to his favorite, Nefertari, and is believed to have fathered more than a hundred children.

Seqenenre Tao 11

He was the next-to-last king of the Seventeenth Dynasty and possibly the father of Kamose, who began the drive to oust the Hyksos from Egypt. The mummy of Seqenenre Tao II reveals gashes to the skull, probably resulting from fierce combat with a Hyksos warrior armed with an ax blade of heavy bronze. The mummy of Seqenenre also shows evidence of a shattered cheekbone and a dagger thrust to the back of its neck.

Thutmose 1

He was the father of Queen Hatshepsut and of her half brother, Thutmose II. He is believed to have been the founder of the walled workers' village on the west bank of the Nile known as Deir el-Medina. As an early ruler of the Eighteenth Dynasty, Thutmose I began the expansion of the boundaries of Egypt that led to the glories of the New Kingdom.

Thutmose 11

He was the husband and half-brother of Queen Hatshepsut. A less prominent pharaoh than his father or his son, Thutmose III (who was not the son of Hatshepsut), was best remembered for having sent a series of military expeditions to the region of Nubia in the south.

Thutmose 111

He was the grandson of Thutmose I, inherited the throne as a child. His aunt and stepmother, Hatshepsut, ruled for twenty years, first as regent and then as queen and "pharaoh" of Egypt. After her death Thutmose III distinguished himself as a great warrior, leading his army deep into Asia. There he lay siege to the stronghold of the Mitanni for seven months before his victory at Megiddo in present-day northern Israel.

Tutankhamen

Today he is the best known of the ancient Egyptian kings, probably because his tomb, which was discovered in 1922, was found almost completely intact. He succeeded the pharaoh Akhenaten, who may have been his father or brother, at the age of nine, and he died at eighteen of unknown but suspicious causes. Although his rule began at Akhetaten, the city built by Akhenaten and dedicated to the worship of the sun disk, Tutankhamen soon moved the capital back to Memphis. The young king was married to one of the daughters of Akhenaten, and the couple is believed to have had two stillborn children.

Zoser

He was the ruler of the Old Kingdom's Third Dynasty, was responsible for a new style in royal burial structures. His Step Pyramid at Sakkara, designed by his architect and vizier, Imhotep, formed a link between the single-story mastaba and the straight-sided pyramids of the Fourth Dynasty. The burial chamber of Zoser's six-stepped pyramid lies underground, beneath the structure.

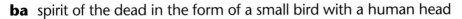

ba spirit of the dead in the form of a small bird with a human head

Book of the Dead spells and prayers to help the deceased on the journey into the afterlife, written on papyrus scrolls or inscribed on tomb walls

canopic jars four jars into which the dried internal organs (liver, lungs, stomach, and intestines) of the deceased were placed for preservation inside the tomb

Coptic the language of Christianized Egyptians consisting of the Greek alphabet and Egyptian vocabulary

dynasty royal family of hereditary rulers

faience blue- or green-glazed quartz-based ceramic used for jewelry and charms as well as for plates and cups

hieroglyphics earliest Egyptian writing, made up of language symbols including pictures, words, and sounds

ka life force, or soul, that would survive death if the body or an acceptable substitute were preserved

kohl paste of crushed mineral, grayish-black or dark green, used to outline the eyes

mastaba a type of tomb in the form of a low rectangular mud brick building with an underground tomb chamber

mummy dead body, human or animal, preserved by natural means or a human–made process

natron salt found in the Egyptian desert, used to dry out the body in the process of mummification

obelisk tapered, four-sided pillar with a pyramidal top, made of a solid block of stone

ostraca limestone chips or broken pottery on which scribes left writings and financial records and on which artists drew sketches

papyrus tall reed from which Egyptians made writing paper, as well as rope, mats, baskets, sandals, and reed boats

scarab dung beetle, Egyptian symbol of eternal life, that inspired jewelry, charms, and seals

shabti small figure of a servant, placed in tombs to do the bidding of the deceased

sphinx a mythical beast; the Great Sphinx at Giza has the body of a lion and the head of a man

Day, Nancy. *Your Travel Guide to Ancient Egypt.* Minneapolis: Runestone/Lerner, 2001.

Harris, Geraldine, and Delia Pemberton. *Illustrated Encyclopedia of Ancient Egypt.* Chicago: Peter Bedrick Books, 1999.

Perl, Lila. *Mummies, Tombs, and Treasure: Secrets of Ancient Egypt.* New York: Clarion/Houghton Mifflin, 1987. Reprint. New York: Scholastic, 1996.

Rossi, Renzo. *The Egyptians: History, Society, Religion.* Hauppauge, New York: Barron's, 1999.

Shuter, Jane. *The Ancient World: Egypt.* Austin, Texas: Raintree Steck-Vaughn,1999.

Time-Life Books: *What Life Was Like on the Banks of the Nile: Egypt 3050-30 B.C.* Alexandria, Virginia: Time-Life, 1996.

Organizations and Online Sites

British Museum
http://www.ancientegypt.co.uk/menu.html
Created by the British Museum, this is a great site to learn more about the culture and history of the ancient Egyptians.

Carnegie Museum of Natural History
4400 Forbes Avenue
Pittsburgh, PA 15213
http://www.clpgh.org/cmnh/exhibits/egypt
On its Web site, this museum features a special section on daily life in ancient Egypt as well as its customs and beliefs.

Detroit Institute of Arts
5200 Woodward Avenue
Detroit, Michigan 48202
http://www.dia.org/collections/ancient/egypt/egypt.html

View artifacts in the institute's collection to learn more about ancient Egyptian culture.

Minnesota State University
http://emuseum.mnsu.edu/prehistory/egypt/

Visit the online exhibit created by students and professors at the Minnesota State University at Mankato. It offers information on archaeology, hieroglyphics, and much more.

Lila Perl has written more than fifty-five books, fiction and nonfiction, mainly for readers in the middle grades and for young adults. Her nonfiction has included social history, family memoir, and biography. She has traveled extensively in Asia, Latin America, and Africa to research material for culture and background studies of more than a dozen countries.

For her research on her first book about ancient Egypt, Ms. Perl spent a month in Egypt as a guest of the government of the late President Anwar el-Sadat, visiting tomb sites and monuments throughout the country and receiving special permission to visit the Mummy Room of the Cairo Museum. Her award-winning book *Mummies, Tombs, and Treasure: Secrets of Ancient Egypt* is available in the original hardcover edition (Clarion/Houghton Mifflin) and in a softcover Scholastic edition.

Two of Lila Perl's books have received American Library Association Notable awards. Nine titles have been selected as Notable Children's Trade Books in the Field of Social Studies. Ms. Perl has also received a *Boston Globe Horn Book* award, a Sidney Taylor Committee award, and a Young Adults' Choice award from the International Reading Association. The New York Public Library has cited several of her titles among its Best Books for the Teen Age.

Lila Perl holds a Bachelor of Arts degree from Brooklyn College and lives in Beechhurst, New York.